Norse Mythology

A Concise Guide to Gods and Beliefs of Norse Mythology

(A Guide Into Norse Gods and Goddesses, Viking Warriors and Magical Creatures)

Alfred Gregory

Published By **Barry Ackles**

Alfred Gregory

All Rights Reserved

Norse Mythology: A Concise Guide to Gods and Beliefs of Norse Mythology (A Guide Into Norse Gods and Goddesses, Viking Warriors and Magical Creatures)

ISBN 978-1-7781462-4-4

No part of this guidebook shall be reproduced in any form without permission in writing from the publisher except in the case of brief quotations embodied in critical articles or reviews.

Legal & Disclaimer

The information contained in this book is not designed to replace or take the place of any form of medicine or professional medical advice. The information in this book has been provided for educational & entertainment purposes only.

The information contained in this book has been compiled from sources deemed reliable, and it is accurate to the best of the Author's knowledge; however, the Author cannot guarantee its accuracy and validity and cannot be held liable for any errors or omissions. Changes are periodically made to this book. You must consult your doctor or get professional medical advice before using any of the suggested remedies, techniques, or information in this book.

Upon using the information contained in this book, you agree to hold harmless the Author from and against any damages, costs, and expenses, including any legal fees potentially resulting from the application of any of the information provided by this guide. This disclaimer applies to any damages or injury caused by the use and application, whether directly or indirectly, of any advice or information presented, whether for breach of contract, tort, negligence, personal injury, criminal intent, or under any other cause of action.

You agree to accept all risks of using the information presented inside this book. You need to consult a professional medical practitioner in order to ensure you are both able and healthy enough to participate in this program.

Table Of Contents

Chapter 1: Norse God Of Death 1

Chapter 2: Thors Wife 15

Chapter 3: Mother Goddess.................... 30

Chapter 4: Goddess Of Love.................... 46

Chapter 5: Mother Of Thor 68

Chapter 6: The Birth Of The Cosmos 81

Chapter 7: The Goddess Of Love And Fertility 89

Chapter 8: The Twilight Of The Gods 104

Chapter 9: The Poetic Tradition 118

Chapter 10: Norse Mythology In Modern Film & Tv-Shows 126

Chapter 11: Viking Age 137

Chapter 12: Teeth Alteration Among Vikings 146

Chapter 13: The Viking Encounter With Christianity 167

Chapter 14: Games And Entertainment 177

Chapter 1: Norse God Of Death

Some human beings sense most sorry for Hel out of Loki's three monster children. Her boys have been scary monsters; however she appeared the maximum like a median individual. Her nice link to lack of existence at the start becomes a bluish pallor and a unhappy face. Later, she was made more macabre. Hel probable wasn't punished as closely as the alternative circle of relatives members because of the reality she wasn't very dangerous. Hel have become taken to a miles off land to serve as a ruler on the identical time due to the fact the rest of her own family were all locked up. Hel lived in the dark, bloodless land of loss of life. She and the arena spherical her were the same in each call and individual. Many famous Norse myths have some component to do with Hel's land. Hel is on the coronary heart of the whole thing, from the primary Ragnarok prophecy to the brutal give up of the fight. But, a few scholars receive as proper with that this wasn't constantly the case. When studying Norse folklore, it is able to be hard to tell the distinction amongst historic beliefs and later writings. Hel, the two-headed goddess, and the location display this.

It turn out to be said that Loki and his lover, Angrboda, had 3 monster kids, and Hel have become a unmarried one in every of them. The gods failed to recognize about Loki and Angrboda's youngsters for a while, but they have been concerned once they ultimately positioned they have been born. Predictions of lousy topics to take area were related to Loki's children. The Prose Edda does now not say masses approximately Angrboda, however it does say that the gods have been scared by way of the use of her participation. The gods proper now determined to take Loki's kids from Jotenheim. They positioned them somewhere more strong to decrease the danger they posed. The snake Jormungandr wasn't quite as massive as he is probably however. He became speedy thrown into the water, but he may additionally get so large that he need to wrap round the arena in time.For a while, the gods sought to tame Fenrir, the wolf. But whilst he had been given too huge and meant to keep in mind, Tyr gave up his proper hand to have bands that couldn't be broken placed round him.Hel regarded the maximum like someone out of the 3. But the gods noticed right away that she become not like extraordinary giantesses.

In later art work, she changed into often proven as going terrible and gross, but the Poetic Edda says that her seems hinted greater lightly at her link to loss of life. The colour of her pores and pores and pores and skin have become a mild blue-gray, and her face modified into continually unhappy.She changed into among Loki's monsters but wasn't as volatile as her animal brothers.

Odin selected that Hel have to be sent away however no longer locked up. Hel modified into despatched very a protracted manner far from Asgard and Midgard, and it became almost not feasible to get to. The dead were given strength over her. The gods have been not punished proper away, in spite of the fact that Loki had stored the births of his kids a secret. Even even though Loki have become a large a part of the Ragnarok predictions, he would possibly now not be caught till after Baldur died.

Many names had been given to Hel's land of loss of life. Many humans concept it have become inside the worldwide for Niflheim. Niflhel became wherein the vain lived on this early global for frost and mist. It have become moreover called Helheim, which means that that "Hel's Home." Eljudnir is sometimes used to consult her corridor at once. But most of the time, Hel's realm is truly referred to as Hel. She dominated over the land of the useless, just like the Greek god Hades did. While Hel wasn't chained like Fenrir, further to Loki would be in the end, her global changed into even though a cage. People stated that her domestic have come to be under considered certainly one of Yggdrasil's large branches, which supposed that she and the individuals who lived in her worldwide could not skip wherein they pleased. The Norse humans believed in a couple of possible afterlife except Hel's worldwide. People's thoughts about the destiny changed, but maximum Norse humans idea that during which someone went after loss of life relied on how they died.

The bravest squaddies who died in battle had been selected to visit Odin's hall for Valhalla or to Folkvangr to be with Freya. Folkvangr turned into later concept moreover to be the house of individuals who died in ideal health however now not in struggle, like girls who died giving begin. People misplaced inside the water have been caught in nets and taken to Aegir's hidden house. They were discovered at the lowest of the seas with the treasures of sunk ships. Most people, even though, died in a exquisite deal much less cute methods. After lack of lifestyles of contamination, vintage age, horrible fulfillment, or hunger, they ended up in Hel. Snorri Sturluson changed his thoughts about Hel in a while. He concept of Hel as a place wherein those who did terrible subjects had been sent because of medieval Christian thoughts approximately punishment and reward within the destiny.

On the alternative hand, humans inside the Norse beyond belief it modified into likely that they might go to Hel's house after dying. The situation did no longer look precise. Hel became a place interior Niflheim which have end up continuously bloodless, foggy, and dark. Even even though it wasn't presupposed to be a penalty, it became a sad and empty region. Hel wasn't endorse to her humans, but. The Prose Edda stated she need to deliver individuals who surpassed some distance from vintage age or illness an area to live and gives, making their unhappy international a bit better.

It wasn't actually those who wound up in Hel's global. One of the most famous memories in Norse legend is about how Loki tricked Baldur's blind brother into beating him with mistletoe, which have become the only element that would harm him. When Baldur died, it broke all the gods' hearts. They planned a huge funeral wherein all the Aesir and Vanir may be present and mourn. Nanna, Baldur's wife, changed into so dissatisfied approximately the loss of life that she surpassed away with unhappiness because the funeral rite started. Her body have turn out to be put on her husband's funeral pyre so that the 2 of them ought to go to Hell collectively. Baldur's mom, Frigg, tried to keep him solid through ordering everything in the Nine Worlds to swear not to harm him. She changed into determined to protect her son, regardless of the fact that she had not noted the mistletoe. She asked the deities to discover a person inclined to make the extended, difficult adventure to Hel. She prayed that Hel might feel sorry for them and permit Baldur pass again to the location that became dwelling.

Hermod stepped up. Odin allow him borrow Sleipnir, his fast horse that might cross among worlds. The adventure took 9 nights, even on Sleipnir. Hermod rode via the darkish until he had been given to a bridge near the brink of Niflheim. As he went down, he reached the locked gates of Hel. Sleipnir jumped over them without trouble, letting Hermod into the sector on the same time as he lived. When Hermod again, the gods went into the Nine Worlds and instructed every dwelling trouble they noticed to weep over Baldur's loss of life. Without fail, all of them did. Even rocks and mountains cried once they notion Baldur might be out of place for precise. They were nearly completed after they came across an elderly big living by myself in a much off part of Jotenheim. They knowledgeable Thokk to cry, but she refused because of the fact she did no longer care about Odin's son and emerge as willing to permit Hel take him. Because Thokk refused to mourn, Baldur have come to be despatched to Hel over suited. The gods might likely preserve being unhappy approximately his loss of life. Sturluson does say that Thokk become probable not what she seemed to be. The grumpy giantess have emerge as concept to be Loki by way of the use of maximum, who desired to ensure that Baldur could not be introduced lower back to existence.

The volva tells Odin that Hel will play a extensive function in her story. Either the deity of the land or the place itself can be what she technique because of the fact each are critical to the quit story. Many of Hel's named characters are related to Ragnarok, as maximum of them display up in Snorri Sturluson's Prose Edda. Much of his writing is ready the sports that led as an lousy lot as the combat, and he used foreshadowing more than a preferred Norse creator need to have.

The seer cautioned Odin that Hel is probably important in Ragnarok. While Snorri Sturluson's story has many more antagonists, Loki and his children have constantly been on the centre of the Ragnarok story. With a few help, they might spoil each the arena of people or the society dominated by way of way of way of the gods. They may prove to be the gods' worst enemies. When Ragnarok started out, the gods could not punish Loki and each three of his children. He ought to stroll out of Niflheim, Fenrir would snap his chains, and Jormungandr might get lower again at the ground. She may bring each one of the deceased people initially despatched to her.

She ought to accumulate a huge military of our our bodies drawn from the Nine Worlds, in which Odin created her as the goddess inside the direction of records.

The demons that have been locked up in conjunction with her should go with her. The frost giants living in Niflheim may be freed, together with Garm and Nidhogg. Based on what we understand about their attack, Loki want to now be alongside collectively together with his daughter's military. He would get to the battleground at the bow of Naglfar, a vessel crafted from the vain humans's arms and toenails. His institution might be customary up of giants, human beings from Hel, and the lifeless. Hel's detail in the battle is in no manner stated, in spite of the fact that her global and the humans living there would possibly play a large aspect in Ragnarok.Hel does now not seem to be within the fight, similar to the gods of the Aesir and Vanir.Hel may also moreover moreover live through

Ragnarok, regardless of the reality that her cherished ones and navy who are dead can be killed.It is written inside the Prose Edda that the area may be rebuilt after the fight. It says that folks that died of Ragnarok and its aftermath might be reborn in new, higher geographical regions. Even even though her name isn't always given, Hel might also nonetheless be accountable for maximum of those destiny afterlife locations.

The call "Hel", for the Norse goddess who kills, comes from some one-of-a-kind sources. She have come to be in fee of a land at the side of her call on it. He is considered one of Loki and Angrboda's 3 children. She and her brothers had been sent away on the same time as the gods positioned out they had been a hazard. She end up installed charge of all the dead while her more younger siblings were chained. Hel's realm come to be normally idea to be in the cold worldwide of Niflheim. It became a sad and dark location. There have been no living matters except the vain and some positive monsters. Still, many famous myths include going to Hel's worldwide. Odin flew there to talk to a volcano, and after Baldur's sudden loss of existence, Hermod tried to make a deal with the goddess.

The occurrences of Ragnarok had been related to most of those stories in a few way. Aside from Loki, Hel failed to seem to be combating herself. Instead, her father led the useless and monsters of Niflheim closer to the gods. Some university college students assume that components of the tale, perhaps even the concept of Hel as a person, had been brought to Norse mythology after the truth. The afterlife become visible as a real region with a god on the helm, prompted via the usage of the use of every Greco-Roman and Christian perspectives. Some people think she appears lots like loss of life deities from one-of-a-kind international locations. In the identical way, they count on Hel modified proper right into a unstable but reliable goddess. We may also in no way apprehend if Hel have turn out to be a real Norse goddess or something made up in medieval writing because the written and archaeological data are gaps.

Chapter 2: Thors Wife

Sif is like many one-of-a-kind characters in Norse mythology: not masses are known approximately them. Even although she end up Thor's companion, not an lousy lot is understood approximately her because of the reality now not many stories do. Sif have emerged as terrific diagnosed for her long, golden hair, which modified into additionally a big a part of her most well-known tale. But even that tale is not in reality about Sif. It's more approximately how her husband reacted when her golden hair changed into stolen. It's additionally concerning what he and the awesome gods were given once they regular that hair. Loki asked the dwarves to make Sif new hair, and moreover they made Thor's, Odin's, and Freyr's maximum well-known objects. Even no matter the truth that not many reminiscences about Sif had been stored alive, what issue she played in Norse mythology continues to be sincerely clean. Many pupils now suppose they and her golden locks had been an awful lot extra outstanding than they will have seemed.

Later writers can also have great seen her due to the fact the spouse of a extra powerful god. However, they left sufficient clues for us to clearly be given as actual with now that Sif changed into married to Thor, the Norse deity of thunder. Norse people notion Thor have emerge as a pretty big god. He emerge as the precept individual in plenty of tales, places and people were named after him, and his well-known awl have become the most recognizable sign of the Viking era. Sif was in all likelihood additionally important due to the fact she end up his partner. But masses extra is thought regarding her husband than approximately her. This is in particular because of the fact there aren't many data of Norse folklore left. Most of what's idea comes from epics written in the thirteenth century. These were referred to as Eddas in Norse and were written numerous centuries after the Viking Age peaked. Most individuals and occurrences within the Eddas occurred most effective inside the Viking Age, as tested inside the survived art work. However, there aren't many written property, so it is hard to get a complete photo of the folklore.

In the Poetic Edda, she indicates up at a dinner party for the gods and is in quick addressed even as her husband talks to Odin. In the Prose Edda, she simplest suggests up speedy inside the story approximately how Loki seized her hair, the only recognized fable together together along with her in it. In this way, we do not realize very an awful lot about Sif. It does now not propose she wasn't a critical goddess surely due to the truth she doesn't display up very regularly within the Eddas. For example, the Prose Edda is normally about how the area have grow to be made and the way it ends.

There had been likely many extra tales that had not some thing to do with the ones activities for the reason that memories regularly had a few element to do with them. In Greek myths, as an example, there were many memories about how the gods got married and had kids. The Norse people may also additionally additionally have advised those recollections, too, but they had been not located down in any resources we recognise in recent times. The memories of a queen like Sif might not have lived on because of the fact that they'd now not something to do with the more violent troubles of what took place spherical Ragnarok. People consider her as Thor's accomplice, but what else she did is unsure. It's no longer even smooth from her name what element she served inside the universe. Even despite the fact that the phrase "Sif" manner "dating," in particular "marriage," it high-quality suggests us that the female become married to one of the historic gods.

Even even though we recognise Sif became married to Thor, there are guidelines internal Eddas that she wasn't usually a devoted and dependable wife. The marriage of Sif and Thor is the identical in the reminiscences surpassed down. Based on the reminiscences we have were given now, Thor seems to be a loving mate. Most tales approximately Sif display her husband shielding her from being slandered or attacked. But there are signs and symptoms that Sif might not be actually as dedicated to Thor. In a Poetic Edda, Loki indicates up in Asgard at a dinner party and makes amusing of all the gods, which makes most of them irritated. Sif remains cool and offers him mead, telling him he can't say a few issue terrible about her because she hasn't finished some component incorrect. Loki, on the other hand, has a horrible phrase for Sif. He stated that he have become the fine character who knew the reality approximately her, which supposed she became dishonest on her husband. He even stated that he changed into in love with Sif. Sif might now not answer this claim.

In earlier elements of the Poetic Edda, it have been hinted that Loki wasn't the most effective individual who knew she end up dishonest on him. When Odin, in cover, refuses to take his son throughout the bay, Thor and Odin insult every other in the same way. In Norse and Celtic cultures, those "flying" conversations were well-known. They were a test of brains and nerve that included insults and smart wordplay. Odin makes amusing of Thor with the resource of pronouncing his partner has a accomplice at domestic on the same time as he's away on one in every of his many adventures. As in step with Thor, the ferryman isn't always telling the truth. He says the false charge is "witless" due to the fact it's far only supposed to harm him and now not be smart. Both gods say that there's a king of fulfillment in the sky. Odin says that via telling the truth, he has tricked

Thor, but Thor won't take note of something he calls mendacity. Other sources, similar to the Prose Edda and shorter songs, do no longer say Sif changed into cheating on his partner. But they may be saying she had a child that wasn't born on the identical time as she married Thor.

Ullr become a god who changed into identified for his magic. It have become said that he led the Aesir if Odin become sent away for a quick time. Several reviews say he's Thor's son-in-law; no character calls him Sif's son's father, and Ullr isn't in any reminiscences. Like his mother, Ullr is one of the gods cited lots sufficient to had been crucial, despite the fact that his memories were out of location. If he's referred to as Sif's son and no longer Thor's son, Sif's story isn't restrained to her marriage with the thunder god. We can inform from the memories that she lived that her non-public lifestyles modified into in all likelihood greater worried than her name by myself, which made it clear that she became his partner.

Sif's maximum famous tale isn't always about a dating or an difficulty. She is better mentioned for her story of strategies Loki took away the detail that made her unique. People stated that Sif have become a adorable queen. Her prolonged, golden hair made her well-known. The Joker reduce off Sif's hair whilst she slept simply to be recommend. It's no longer clear how Loki got here so near Sif at the same time as she turn out to be dozing in the story. Some human beings see this as evidence that Loki emerge as her lover, due to the fact the poet Edda stated, on the identical time as others assume he drugged Sif and Thor to drag off his comic story.

Loki generally positioned a manner to get out of his problems. This time, he stated that the gnomes may also need to deliver Sif new hair. The expert metalworkers need to make hair out of actual gold that became even greater lovable than the hair he had stolen. It changed into good enough for Loki to make a experience to Svartalfheim, the dwarves' basement home, to get Sif new hair. But if Loki failed, Thor could preserve his word and treat Loki severely for attacking his accomplice. A organization of dwarves in Svartalfheim, amazing referred to as the "sons of Ivaldi", agreed to do what Loki requested. They created Sif, a crown of golden threads that might broaden on her head like herbal hair. Loki wasn't pleased with this, but. He attempted his achievement as commonly. This time, although, the very last effects might be top for the gods.

He went to the dwarves' land to have themselves make Sif new hair, however he got here again to Asgard with many one of a kind offers for the gods. They attempted to win over Asgard with the useful useful resource of making even greater high-quality magical topics. They gave these to

Loki so he should deliver them to the gods for Asgard whilst he returned. Loki already again from Svartalfheim with masses greater than everybody concept he need to. But he determined the notable manner to win lower again the gods' favour became to carry lower back even better subjects. He approached every exclusive tribe of dwarves and confirmed them what Ivaldi's sons had made. He wager them that they couldn't healthy the attraction and capability that went into them. A pair of brothers, Brokkr and Sindri, took up that assignment. Loki made the guess volatile thru telling the two brothers that they will chop off his head if they received. Loki changed proper right right into a fly to get their hobby far from their artwork, however Brokkr and Sindri nevertheless made extraordinary topics for Loki to offer to the gods. Loki added five terrific gives with him on the same time as he all over again to Asgard, on the facet of Sif's new hair.

Loki gave the ones items to Odin, Thor, and Freyr. They gladly took them in. Loki's shaggy dog tale did now not trouble Thor due to the fact Sif desired her new hair. Loki had said that Sif's new golden hair may be extra adorable than the antique one. Freyr stored Skiðblaðnir as well as the golden pig for himself. Odin took the spear and the ring for himself. Thor claimed Mjollnir along with his spouse's golden hair. In Asgard, the hammer would be the best tool that made him stand out. Indeed, Mjollnir wasn't perfect. When Brokkr and Sindri went to Asgard to get their prize, Loki's head, he informed them that that that they had lessen the control a chunk too quick due to the truth they were sidetracked through way of a fly biting them. Even even though Mjollnir had this minor flaw, Thor stated it end up nevertheless as precious as the opportunity works. Loki become most effective able to preserve his calm thru using smart words. The dwarves even sewn his mouth close so he could not use his smarts to trick human beings over again.

Historiographers have a first rate concept of what Sif may additionally furthermore have finished within the Norse Pantheon based totally completely totally on her lengthy, golden hair. Many historians assume that Sif is one of the oldest gods in the Pantheon. They bear in mind she and Ullr play smaller additives in later recollections due to the truth human beings have already forgotten about them. Instead, they have been greater well-known in the past, perhaps even earlier than titans like Odin and Thor have come to be famous. As a cease end result, many humans think that Sif is a part of one of the oldest legendary beings. Stories that have been passed down and the poetry of the time of the Viking skalds be a part of Sif's golden hair to steel. However, the proper word is likewise used at the same time as discussing wheat and in addition grains. As a end result, many human beings keep in mind Sif as a goddess of fertility and plant life.

Historiographers have located proof of this in both writings about Sif and her husband's cult. People recognise Thor as a fighter and the god of thunder, but inside the Norse World, he modified into moreover visible as a discern god. People used amulets formed like his famous hammer, Mjollnir, to hold them secure. There is also proof that that they had some component to do with getting pregnant. To make sure a remarkable crop, hammer or awl-ordinary tokens were at times buried inside the preliminary seeds sown in the spring, even after the time of the Vikings. In exquisite myths, there may be moreover a sturdy link amongst a thundering god and a fertility lahs. Many vintage religions married their fertility goddesses to their sky gods due to the fact rain makes the fields fertile and permits flowers develop.

In Norse mythology, Sif's element continuously connects to that of her husband Thor. Her call alone makes it easy that she is mounted to a person with the useful resource of marriage, not non-public inclinations. But despite the fact that, Sif modified into in all likelihood an important god in its personal right. Most probably, the shortage of unique memories about her is due to the reality there are not many property left. The testimonies which have been advised approximately her hint that she cheated on her husband, but most of the time, they're informed thru his aid of her. When Odin, pretending to be a ferryman, talks about her affair, Thor calls them a liar.

In a single story, Loki says he is in love with Sif. Some readers nowadays expect that is how he were able to famously stealing Sif's hair at the same time as she changed into drowsing. Loki had strands of proper gold created through dwarves installation Sif's hair as an alternative. He additionally delivered lower lower back other unique provides for the celestial beings and earned their forgiveness via manner of manner of demonstrating their quality tendencies. Many pupils assume that Sif's hair represents wheat. They say that this gives her a goddess of delivery. In this, her marriage to Thor is an integral part of the story. Together, they suit a famous delusion about a marriage between an earth queen and a sky god who brings rain to the earth. In the beyond, the story of Sif's hair may also moreover have been used to provide an purpose at the back of why wintry weather got here after the grain turn out to be lessen. But like masses of her tales, this one come to be a delusion approximately Thor and how he have been given his well-known hammer.

Chapter 3: Mother Goddess

Some pantheons located gods and women on nearly the equal degree. When the Greeks perception approximately gods, they frequently positioned them together in pairs based on gender. However, the Norse Pantheon modified into now not cut up up as pretty as a few. There are numerous reminiscences and superpowers about many gods, however now not lots is notion regarding most of the gods and goddesses. You can fine find out Frigg in a few Norse myths, however she constitutes one of the maximum vital ones. She grow to be the most muscular goddess most of the Aesir because of the truth she changed into Odin's wife. But her technique changed into extra than truly being a wife. Frigg turned into a robust goddess in herself. Her stories showcase how she seemed out for her youngsters, which made her an excellent opponent for her husband.

Like maximum ancient Norse gods, Frigg does not have a story about how she got here to be. On the opportunity hand, historians can find a story approximately how her man or woman got here to be. The Germanic gods have been called Aesir. When humans from Central Europe went to Denmark and Scandinavia in the course of the time of the Vikings, they delivered these items. Frig has been written down in almost all the Germanic languages that we realize of. In Old German, the Saxons named her Fri, and in Old English, she turned into called Frig. These names all come from the equal a part of the language. The proto-Germanic word *Frijjo originated as a woman phrase that meant "loved." It is likewise the deliver of the word "loose."It's difficult to say how comparable the testimonies regarding the ones goddesses were due to the fact maximum societies do now not have many written information. Hers is among severa names that sound alike, suggesting that European human beings had similar mind approximately the gods. One instance is that the determine is said to be married to the area version of Odin in almost all testimonies.

For example, in a German ballad from the 1100s, Woden and Frija paintings together to heal Balder's horse. Balder is their son. Even greater simply, the tale of approaches the Germanic Langobards in northern Italy came to expose the relationship. Their tale stated that the Vandals were after a small group led through a woman known as Gambara. When the Vandals known as to "Godan" for assist, he knowledgeable them that he may additionally need to choose the person he noticed first factor within the morning. In the intervening time, Gambara's children prayed to Frea, Godan's partner. She knowledgeable them that the girls within the organization need to tie their hair to their faces and pose with the men on the equal time as the sun comes up. Frea moved his bed to stand Gambara's tribe while

Godan slept. He idea the small institution have come to be an lousy lot extra large because of the reality the women gave the look of men with beards, so he gave them the decision Langobards, this means that "Long-Beards."From as a ways away as Italy, the tale demonstrates that Odin's spouse become a goddess who modified into masses like ours. She saved the relationship going and kept up her photograph as a loving goddess.

Frigg is frequently taken into consideration a mom goddess because of her function and the manner she turned into described. In many Indo-European cultures, the partner of the primary god is kind of a mom. For example, Hera modified into the Greek goddess of marriage and own family because of the truth she have become married to Zeus. This is how most people see Frigg. As a associate of the All-Father, she emerge as like a mom discern, despite the fact that few gods have been referred to as their kids in most stories. This symbolic hyperlink is taken more extensively within the Prose Edda.

Baldur turned into nearly absolutely safe from harm because of the reality Frigg ensured her son have become stable. The special gods threw various things at him as a pastime and watched as they swerved within the air to save you hitting him. Loki turned into inquisitive about how Baldur is probably saved steady whilst he noticed this activity. He placed on an antique woman's garments and requested Frigg the query without any trouble. He furthermore found she had forgotten simplest one issue inside the Nine Worlds at the same time as she made her ensures. Even even though the mistletoe near Valhalla hadn't promised Baldur protection, she failed to anticipate a good buy of it as it have become the type of small plant.

When Loki found a threat, he used that mistletoe to make an arrow. He gave it to

Hodr to avoid being caught. Hodr wasn't as fortunate as Baldur, a beautiful and nicely-preferred god. He were blind when you bear in mind that begin and come to be in no way allowed to take part in lots of Asgard occasions, collectively with this sport. Loki gave Hodr an arrow simply so he have to take part. Even the blind god requested him to help him purpose it due to the fact Hodr could not see his aim. The shot hit Baldur right within the chest and killed him proper away. Loki were given away in advance than he may be blamed. When their maximum appreciated pal died, the gods were saddened. Frigg, mainly, became complete of disappointment. She asked the gods, in tears, if any of them ought to go to Hel. She was hoping they'll get the goddess who watched over the vain to allow Baldur pass from her realm.

Hermod, who some property say is Frigg's 0.33 son, took at the quest. He took Sleipnir to embark on the prolonged, tough enjoy to the dark worldwide of lack of life. Hel agreed to allow Baldur flow into as long as all residing topics at the Nine Worlds cried to show that they loved and disregarded him as a good deal as the Aesir stated. The gods went to all of the worlds and asked all the dwelling things there to be unhappy about Baldur's loss of life. Every rock and mountain cried once they heard Frigg's son might be misplaced all of the time. In Jotenheim, even though, one giantess may not cry. So Hel refused to permit Baldur to move; Thokk, who changed into probably Loki dressed up, did no longer show any sadness. Later memories display that Frigg continues to be sad about the dying of her son. Frigg said the trickster could have been killed proper away if she had a boy like Baldur in the room at the same time as Loki stopped a banquet. Finally, the gods may pay Loki a excessive rate for Baldur's death with the useful resource of tying him. For Frigg, Baldur's lack of life modified into her first sadness. The subsequent occasion is probably Odin's lack of lifestyles at Ragnarok, which changed into positive to expose up.

Frigg had friends besides her husband and kids, but. In Norse folklore, the gods had been mainly cut up into companies: the Aesir and the Vanir. The goddesses, alternatively, had been greater numerous. Not first-rate humans born into those groups but furthermore jotnar and elves were said to be among them. People idea that Frigg changed into the most important goddess. Freya have become the only character who came near to appearing as effective and authoritative as she emerge as. Frigg is regularly shown because of the truth the maximum important of the asynjur, or gods. She became the most critical female in her humans, like an historical queen along side her courtroom docket women spherical her.

Even although Frigg come to be usually visible with Odin, she end up thoughtful sufficient to have an area. She resided in Fensalir, a lovable region with marshes and ponds. With the gods that served her there, Fensalir have become probable a totally girly location. Fulla and Frigg were particularly near and hard to cut up. Other gods with comparable names, like Volla, are frequently visible inside the equal manner, so she additionally appears to originate from a preceding Germanic tradition. Folke's most important system have turn out to be to hold an ash-wood subject that belonged to Frigg. It emerge as given an air of mystery of significance no matter the fact that nobody knew what turn out to be inner. People knew Fulla and Frigg were associated because of the reality they were both gift at Baldur's lack of life. When Hermod were given lower lower back from Hel, he had gives from Baldur's partner, Nanna, who had passed away at some degree inside the funeral employer from sadness. Nanna sent Fulla a ring alongside facet a few adorable linens for her mom-in-law. Even despite the fact that Frigg's helpers had been now not as extensively recognized, they were but professional as goddesses of their personal right. People like Fulla have been now not best one of the gods' pals and helpers however moreover extensions of her strength and effect.

Another famous story approximately Frigg proves that she cared about extra than actually her son as a mother. In one story, younger kings have been fishing close to their domestic after they were swept into the sea. They washed up at the shore near the house of an vintage farmer couple that took them in. The older man cared for Geirroth, the younger boy, at the same time as his partner cared for Agnar, the larger brother. The guy warned the boys it modified into time to move again to their father's land after a 365 days and gave the ones humans a supply to help them get there. However, he pulled Geirroth away and whispered a few issue to him in advance than they left. He left the canoe early whilst the guys have been given near home. Then he threw it once more into the water alongside together with his sibling though interior. He said he was hoping this went to an evil ghost. When Geirroth have been given back domestic, he determined that his dad had died at the same time as he changed into away. His family member, cited to have lived, come to be the only individual who became made king. He changed into best nine years vintage. Odin and Frigg observed every boys get greater big. Of route, the antique pair had raised them and come to be however inquisitive about their former expenses.

Agnar became caught on the coast of a wildland and lived in a cave. She was a giantess, and Odin become proud that his adoptive son have turn out to be developing up to be a notable king. Frigg responded that Geirroth changed into impolite and suggest and will possibly have tortured a traveler in location of sharing his wealth. Odin made a wager to reveal that Frigg's claim changed into no longer valid. To get to Geirroth's hall, he decrease returned to Midgard dressed as a magician. Frigg changed into lying whilst she stated what she did, but she stated it due to anger to protect her observed son. But she did not need to lose her pledge to Odin, so she brought Fulla for King Geirroth in advance than he left Asgard. Fulla warned Geirroth that a wizard would possibly come to his court to curse him and sweep away the united states.

When Odin showed up and called him Grimnir, Geirroth grabbed him. He positioned him thru eight nights of torture to get them to admit that he turn out to be planning to thieve from him. As a traveller, Grimnir did not get any care until the 9th night time, at the same time as Geirroth's son, who changed into named after Agnar, gave him a drink of ale to make him experience higher. Even despite the fact that Frigg wasn't named after the tune, she became the betwinner. Agnar was the most effective person who became kind to Odin, even though it emerge as a separate Agnar from the only Frigg had blanketed. Trickery end up used to get her to do it, despite the fact that, which suggests how strongly protecting Frigg is. To shield her adopted son from being lied about, she may additionally even prison and torture her husband.

Freya turn out to be the simplest god who have grow to be as effective and essential as Frigg. There may also moreover were a first rate motive for the Vanir goddess to be so near the powerful Aesir queen. Scholars have concluded that Frigg and Freya might have been extraordinary components of a single goddess. The Aesir and Vanir spirits had been considered to return from awesome societies for a long term. When Germanic humans came to Scandinavia, every of them took over. They got rid of the gods which have been already there from older cultures. One evidence for this concept is that the Vanir demons do now not appear to have any linguistic or mythological contrary numbers in severa Germanic cultures. Folks global take transport of as real with in Odin, Frigga, Thor, and other Aesir gods, however fine in Scandinavia do the Vanir seem. That might not be the case with Freya, however.

The names Frigg and Freya sound alike, no matter the fact that they arrive from top notch root phrases. It's smooth to peer how Fri or Frijja can also additionally connect to Frigg and Freya, in particular in different Germanic nations. There have been moreover a few similarities in how they labored. The Norse gods' lands had been in no manner as easy as in a few one-of-a-type cultures, but Frigg and Freya were connected to marriage, girls, and having youngsters. Most of the time, Frigg, in Norse folklore, is visible because the goddess of motherhood, union, and circle of relatives.

This is particularly due to the truth she is married to Odin. All the celestial beings and people who referred to as him "All-Father" noticed her as their mother because of the truth she became his spouse. The tales approximately Frigg stress her role as a mother.

When it changed into said that her son Baldur might die, Frigg did the whole lot she may additionally additionally need to to maintain him stable. When her efforts fell, and he end up sent to Hel, she became unfortunate, and her grief confirmed in later memories. Frigg might also need to even combat collectively in conjunction with her husband due to the fact she changed into a protecting mother figure. When Odin said his stepson changed into more succesful than hers, Frigg improved events or even punished Odin to win their guess. There is not any doubt that Frigg is a Germanic decide. Records in the course of Europe talk about goddesses with the identical names, connections, and roles. Some historians suppose she might have been connected to a form best found in Scandinavia. Most human beings count on that Freya does now not have a Germanic parallel. However, enough similarities among her and Frigg make some people expect they may have come from the same area.

Chapter 4: Goddess Of Love

Freya, due to this "woman" in Old Norse, changed into the call of the Norse goddess for romance. She looked for love and satisfaction, however she modified right into a complex man or woman So strong modified into she to the Vikings that they noticed her as a goddess on a degree with Odin and Thor in Norse folklore. Most human beings apprehend Freya, furthermore written as Freyja, Freja, Froja, or Frøya, as a goddess of affection, however she changed into moreover in rate of start, warfare, and lack of life. Through her legend, we examine her critical feature in each element of sexuality. But it looks as if she wasn't allowed to do some thing related to childbirth, which one-of-a-kind goddesses of the same kind were allowed to do. She became in all likelihood a good sized determine in early Nordic faith due to the reality she emerge as associated with the start of life. One of her most important jobs modified into to deliver half of of of the fallen soldiers who died within the warfare to her grand palace in Folkvangar. Odin have to have picked the opportunity 1/2 and brought them to Valhalla. Who grow to be decided on via manner of the use of which god seemed to rely upon how famous the vain hero have become.

Freya emerge as associated with a number of excellent inclinations and things. For her, pigs have been holy. She rode a boar further to drove a carriage pulled via manner of the usage of cats. It modified into moreover said that she had a coat, cape, or dress made from falcon feathers. Freya modified into additionally associated with witchcraft, and some myths say that she taught the Viking Aesir gods a way to do it. An antique Norse poem called Hyndluljóð names the animal Hildisvíni, proving it became a pig. It changed into stated that her brother Freyre had a pig named Gullinborsti. Freya became also associated with horses via using manner of H. R. Ellis Davidson, who says that the goddess had a completely unique relationship with horses and saved them in her holy places.

She additionally had a necklace referred to as Brísingamen that had some issue to do with the naughty god Loki. In the 1300s and 1400s, late Old Norse texts said that the chain belonged to Freya. People say the selection approach "necklace of the Brisings," however I'm now not certain what which means that. Some suppose the necklace's name comes from the Norwegian phrase brisa, due to this shrine. Some humans anticipate it'd have a few aspect to do with the phrases "Brosinga mene" from the poem "Beowulf."There have been 4 exceptional names for Freya: Mardoll, Horn, Gefn, and Sýr. Sometimes, the call Sýr way "sow," however it can moreover suggest "to defend" or "shield." The name Horn originates from the Old Norse word Horr, which means that "flax" or "linen."In Scandinavian society, linen changed right

right into a sacred commodity that become idea to preserve evil away and bring fertility. This can be the hyperlink between the two. Making flax have become a hobby for ladies, and it was regularly linked to weddings because marriage apparel were made from linen. In the equal manner, Gefn manner "giver" in Old Norse. There are clean ties to Freya's obligations proper right here; she brings love and existence.

Freya became from a family of Vanir Gods who have been in fee of maximum pregnancy-related subjects. People say she had an same dual brother in charge of the harvest. Njord, the god who created the sea, turned into her father. He modified into in rate of the sea, the wind, and cash. People said that Njord lived in Nóatún, located by using the water. Freyre is her dual brother. He modified into furthermore born into the Vanir tribe, however the Aesir gave him the land of Alfheim as a present, wherein he lives. Some people have great thoughts about who her parent changed into. Some records say she might have been Njord's unknown sister. Some say her mother had been Nerthus, who modified into like Mother Earth in Norse mythology. Some say that her mother turned into Njord Skadi's daughter and his companion.

Freya become conceived right right into a own family of gods referred to as Vanir. They lived in a place known as Vanaheim. But there can be a tale about how she switched to the other employer of gods, the Aesir, to whom Thor and Odin belonged. After this transformation, she and her husband Ódr lived in Asgard, like Mount Olympus in Greek mythology. There are particular reminiscences approximately who her accomplice turned into and the way he could have been associated with Odin, much like there were taken into consideration considered one of a kind tales approximately her mom. Some human beings say that Freya is the identical individual as Odin's spouse, Figg, and the 2 are frequently considered the same. Some property do no longer list Ódr; as an opportunity, they listing Freyre as Freya's husband. Snorri Sturluson, an Icelandic author who wrote the most whole e-book on Norse folklore, moreover lists Ódr as her husband.

They stated that that they had ladies, one named Hnoss and the alternative named Gersemi. Both in their names mean "treasure." It is outstanding stated that they'll be Freya's kids, and now not whatever else is belief approximately their lives. Even so, the reality that their names are linked to treasure can be associated with Freya's picture in myths as a prize that can be acquired or demanded. It moreover pertains to the tale that Freya cried gold tears.

Freya is referred to in lots of memories that come from Old Norse texts. Some testimonies say that Freya searched the world for her missing husband and cried golden tears. This tale has been round because of the fact that as a minimum the tenth century. In a few exclusive story, she modified from a god from the Aesir extended circle of relatives to a god from the Vanir tribe. This happened due to the Aesir-Vanir War, which began out out due to the truth the Aesir and Vanir had been hostile in the direction of every unique, and their cultures differed. As a form of collateral, Freya, the more youthful Freyre, and their dad have been sent to the Aesir once they ultimately got here to a deal.

The Aesir in the end embraced the 3 to be in reality considered considered one of their personal. Freya short taught an Aesir god to apply seidr, an antique Norse form of magic. Freya changed into furthermore a volva, or "seeress," and had been part of an business agency agency of ladies who've been seers or shamans. They used seidr magic, likely the most organized type of magic within the worldwide of the Norse. Norse myths say that Freya have been the primary person to expose this art work to the historic gods earlier than imparting it to people.

As part of the art work of seidr, human beings used magic to figure out what would possibly arise after which labored with destiny to make topics distinct. People who practised seidr attempted to make new subjects arise in the international. The seer can also need to think about any manner to apply this power. This can be completed to make horrible topics occur, like getting unwell or having lousy properly fortune, or even to harm or harm someone. Plus, it may be used for such things as getting better, winning a combat, or finding hidden subjects.

During Norse times, those human beings may also waft at some point of the land doing magic for folks that paid them for food or a place to stay. Like many folks that used magic for the duration of statistics, a seeress or sorceress had a vague social position. Freya have emerge as feared with the aid of way of some for her capabilities and wanted for by means of manner of the use of others. There is proof that Freya gave this artwork to the gods in the Ynglinga Saga, written with the aid of the Icelandic creator and creator Snorri Sturluson in 1225, and in the Eddas, medieval Icelandic books. Also, future is a massive a part of thousands Norse folklore.

In taken into consideration one of his Eddic songs, Loki says that Freya slept with all of the gods and elves, even her family. Loki and Freya's chain Brisingamen are also a part of some other story. Many texts do no longer talk the tale a good buy; they are saying that Loki stole Brisingamen. The additives about Loki's position are most effective available in portions, so the whole narrative modified into out of place to time.

In a few memories, Heimdall and Loki combat over the chain even as dressed as seals! Some recollections moreover say that Heimdall introduced the necklace. Another tale about the necklace says Freya slept with four gnomes to get it lower once more. In many tales, she is the item of preference. In one story, the big Thrym use her as a bargaining chip. He says he's going to handiest supply Thor all over again the hammer he stole if he gets Freya for himself. This is how Freya seems in hundreds of Norse myths: because the "fee" of things. Many myths useful resource the concept that Freya have been reachable whilst used as rate. There are also many recollections approximately Freya and Giants. For example, one tale talks about how a large provided to assemble partitions round Asgard. Freya, the sun, and the moon have been the reimbursement for what he requested for. In a fantastic tale, a massive named Hrungnir stated he might bypass Valhalla with Jotunheimen, sink Asgard.

According to a few Old Norse writings which have been preserved, Freya and Frigg are one-of-a-kind spirits. But some things about them are the equal and are absolutely really worth noting. Daniel McCoy says that those variations can be defined via way of the truth that the Norse have been engaged in making Frigg and Freya, one-of-a-type ladies from the same Germanic goddess, at the same time as Iceland and Scandinavia have emerge as Christian. It does not appear like there could have been a church of Freya, however many humans in Norway and Sweden count on the names of many places are connected to her. Frøihov and Frłvi are examples. These times make it easy that human beings apprehend Freya impacts their lives.

Idunn: Goddess of Youth

In Norse mythology, Idunn is an essential god. People accept as actual with she is a deity of youngsters, growth, and the precious apples of lifestyles. The tale of

Idunn and her apples shows how critical it become in Norse legend to live younger for all time and be afraid of having vintage. She is the apple keeper, representing how existence is going in cycles and the manner her magic makes the gods experience better. Norse folklore frequently talks about or tells Idunn's story thru the eyes of different characters. As a goddess of immortality, more youthful people, rebirth, and often growth, Iðunn cared for the mystical apples that stored the gods younger and alive forever. She took them collectively at the side of her in a container termed an eski.

People say that Idunn is a quite woman with extended golden hair. She is excellent regarded for her fruit, which a few anticipate presentations her beauty and kids. There are many ideas approximately Iðunn because of the fact her memories are spread out in unique mythologies. Idunn has tied the knot to Bragi, the god of poetry and skalds. This makes a connection amongst telling reminiscences and living all the time. She is well-known for being the main character inside the Haustlong tale, in which Loki, the devious God, hints Iþunn into going to the large Thjazi to steal holy apples.

Idunn's name has multiple meanings, however all of them relate to her magical ability to stay more youthful forever. Her call comes from Old Norse and manner "The Rejuvenating One" or "Giver of Eternal Youth." This emphasizes even extra that she is in fee of the gods' existence. Idunn come to be the high-quality one that need to take care of and offer her golden apples. It says in the Haustlong that Iðunn turn out to be the "maiden who knew the everlasting lifestyles of the Aesir."The accurate manner to write down Idunn is «unn, and the proper way to say it's miles "IH-dune." Today, we do now not have the letter Eth in English, so her name is often written as Idun, Idunn, Ithun, or perhaps Iduna.

The goddess Idunn is answerable for existence after lack of lifestyles, restoration, more youthful human beings, and fertility. Because she nice indicates up a few times in legend, little else is aware of approximately her; except, she can be able to make gods immortal and more youthful all the time. She is likewise referred to as the goddess of limitless spring due to the reality she is idea to keep you young forever and heal you. Also, this has something to do collectively together with her golden apples, which provide the gods limitless younger human beings and life. There are special critiques on wherein Idunn's magical apples were given their power. Some say they got here from her apples, at the same time as others say Idunn herself had the skills. Some humans assume that the text talks approximately apples in severa memories. In evaluation, others say that "Idunn apples" were a few one-of-a-type fruit and that medieval Christian authors introduced apples to make the narrative of Genesis wholesome better.

The Aesir and Vanir are now and again hard to differentiate due to the reality their versions are not continually obvious. People say that the Vanir prize nature, magic, and peace, whilst the Aesir cost strength, strength, and war. Some people idea that Iðunn have become an Asynjur, a deity of the Aesir, even though her powers resembled those of the Vanir. She cared for them, so it made feel that she become additionally part of them!

We do not know an entire lot approximately Idunn past the tales she's been in, so we do not recognize lots approximately her close to family, who're regularly neglected or most effective addressed in short. The maximum vital man or woman in Idunn's family is her husband, Bragi, the god of poems and skalds. There is a purpose why the deity of poetry and the goddess of existence have been given married. In Norse society, poetry and recollections have been important techniques to honour one's existence and movements, and that they have been regularly seen as a manner to stay all the time. Through Bragi's tales, many celestial beings discover their way to stay all the time.

Bragi became furthermore the god of tune, and he grow to be said to have a lovely voice and be first-rate at gambling the harp. His task grow to be to apply his poetry and musical compositions to welcome useless fighters to Valhalla. People say that he has a long beard and that runes are carved into his tongue. There also are one in every of a kind testimonies approximately in which Bragi came from. Some say he was Odin's son, at the equal time as others say Odin had been so taken together together with his song and poems that he made him a god. People observed him because of the fact the wintry climate god for leisure because of the truth his recognition on a laugh went nicely with the stop of flora and the begin of wintry weather.

We do now not realize who Idunn's circle of relatives is, but her powers are associated with those of various Aaesir goddesses from Norse folklore. Like Frigg and Freyja, she is a begin goddess and is considered a part of the energy that works behind the scenes. People count on that her skills can also have come from Frigg and Freyja and that she grew from the recollections of these goddesses. In Idunn's tale within the Lokasenna, which is a part of what is known as the Poetic Edda, Loki insults her by means of way of pronouncing that she slept with the person that killed her brother. As prolonged as this tale is spherical, we do not recognize who Idunn's brother is or why Bragi may be blamed for killing him.

We pleasant know a few things approximately Idunn: she has magic and may be very innocent; she is best stated in short or as part of a larger story. Most of the data we've got were given determined out approximately her became out of place to time, however the fact that she had one of the maximum robust powers of all the Norse deities and goddesses. In the same manner, distinctive figures, which consist of Sif, the deity of harvest, have their powers, households, and roles referred to as into query.

The occasions befell even as Loki, Odin, and Hoenir had been on a searching excursion. They have been on the point of consume once they observed out the hearth that that they had constructed would not cook dinner dinner the ox's meat. As Újazi, a huge eagle, watched them fail at cooking the beef, he made them a suggestion: if they gave him the initial bites of the ox, he'd help them prepare dinner dinner it. The gods agreed, and Újazi flew all the manner all of the manner all the way down to consume the ox. Loki were given mad at Újazi for consuming masses and rammed his personnel thru the eagle's body. As if Újazi could not permit pass of his body of workers, he flew into the environment with Loki and begged Loki to assist them steal Idunn and her golden apples in pass again for his lifestyles.

Loki attempts to get Iðunn to depart by means of the use of way of telling her he noticed an apple of gold within the wooded location out of doors Asgard after being freed. As fast as she had been given there, Azaz swooped down like an eagle to grab her and take her to his vicinity of start in Jotunheim, the land known as Jotnar. He stole her holy apples. Once she changed into long gone, the deities of Asgard commenced to grow antique in regular techniques. They speedy observed this change and perception Loki need to had been as plenty as something, in order that they arrested Loki. Now that the plan is obvious, Loki threatens to kill Idunn if he does no longer pass decrease again him.

Loki stole Freyja's feathers and have become a hawk. He then flew at some point of the land to Jotunheim. He decided Idunn on my own in Jazi's house because it appeared like he became fishing. She became clean for him to take because he ought to flip her right right into a nut. He then took her and lower decrease returned to Asgard. For your facts, the Prose Edda could no longer say that Þjazi stole the apples or that Loki gave them once more. This is a fantastic, exciting piece of proof for the concept that Idunn's apples did no longer have any energy and that she have become the handiest who become given the ability to live extra youthful forever.

Loki ran back to Asgard quick, however it did now not recollect variety due to the reality Þjazi again from his trip and located that Idunn wasn't there. He moreover flies to Asgard, but the gods already have some detail deliberate. The gods set a lure for Þjazi due to the fact he became coming.

When Loki and Idunn had been given off the boat, they lit fireplace to an accumulation of wood shavings they'd located inside the eagle's manner. Þjazi couldn't trade his course, so he crashed into the fireside and fell to the floor. The gods killed him, and Idunn have end up added back.

We've already stated there are particular opinions on whether or now not Idunn had whatever to do with apples. One thing to think about is that specific myths and beliefs probably affected the telling of Norse memories. In Greek mythology and Germanic and Anglo-Saxon folklore, apples are often associated with new existence and renewal. But apples and signs that talk over with them had been decided within the path of archaeological digs.

There is likewise a legendary link among apples and shipping, that is each other purpose to assume that Idunn changed into the usage of apples. But awesome property say that Idunn's powers also can have fashioned a part of her, just like the ones of other fertility goddesses, and that the apples have been a sign of them. This will likely purpose masses speculation thinking about the fact that we do not know masses about Idunn except the 2 instances she shows up within the legend. But one element is excessive nice: Idunn has modified our thoughts about Norse myths.

Chapter 5: Mother Of Thor

Many gods or their households are not frequently referred to inside the Viking texts that have survived, but Thor's mom is pointed out masses. People generally called her a giantess, and her name became Jord. There are not any facts in their connection, however she have become paired with Odin in the end, and they had his most famend son. Even no matter the fact that she has the ones widespread ties, Jord in no manner indicates up as her man or woman. In not one of the recollections does she talk or perhaps show up at vast sports activities as she does? Despite this, a few historians despite the fact that assume that Jord end up a big determine in older mythology. Some humans assume that Jord might have been a chief Germanic mother goddess in the beyond, notwithstanding the reality that no person knows her tale. This is because of the symbolic importance of her given name and her son's call.

A lot of Old Norse property say that Jord is Thor's mom. Many humans call her a jotunn, due to this "giantess." In Norse reminiscences, this phrase did no longer imply both length or man or woman. It is stated that many Jotnar girls joined Aesir gods or had children with them. People of each races had those sorts of relationships all of the time, which confirmed that there wasn't a whole lot difference a number of the girls. And the truth that Jord indicates up on a few lists of goddesses backs this up. There become now not something weird about her detail, no matter the truth that she became a giantess. The legend of strategies Jord and Odin had Thor isn't suggested in any myths that have been exceeded down. Compared to the Greeks and Romans, the Norse human beings did no longer write a whole lot about their gods' every day lives and dramas. Odin were given hitched to Frigg, but he had as a minimum one infant in Jord at some point. It changed into Thor, the sturdy and well-known thunder god.

Jord's name is one of the most well-known in Norse folklore. "Jord's son" is another name for Thor, and she or he or he's said as one in each of Frigg's warring parties collectively with the alternative moms of Odin's sons. What makes her unique is that multiple resources deliver a easy own family tree. In Norse mythology, many figures, even vital gods, did no longer have such information. A giantess whose given call supposed "Night" became said to have been Jord's mother within the Prose Edda. Her father grow to be the second husband of this giantess, and her grandpa come to be Narfi, who turn out to be Night's father. Some memories say that a selected lady is Thor's mother. Even so, really every person sees eye to eye that most of those are surely incredible names for Jord and no longer very well awesome humans. Even even though her name is used often and her son is famous, not a good deal else is understood approximately Jord in the surviving reminiscences. Her name turn out to be given to her as a goddess, however no myths say she spoke or became a substantial prevalence with extraordinary gods.

The significance of her name is one cause there are such a lot of first-hand debts of Jord. Jord is a phrase which means that "earth" or "soil." So, it's far often hard for researchers to tell which assets are speaking about the goddess and which are not. Some components might be speakme about the land in a broader sense. It's now not really that the which means that of Jord's name is tough to translate. It can also be a connection with an older Norse folklore story. Odin's partner is normally named Frigg, a goddess in price of households and giving start. Four of his sons were born to Frigg. Baldur and Hodr were his boys. Even even though Baldur changed into appreciated, he never have become as robust or famous as Thor. Textual and archaeological data display that Thor have end up one of the Pantheon's most reliable and worshipped gods. Some students anticipate this is probably due to the fact Thor end up as soon as taken into consideration Odin's genuine heir.

In older variations of the memories, they count on that Jord have become Odin's partner. As mythology grew and changed, the deity of the land have become substituted with the resource of a mom determine who changed into extra home and properly-informed. There is some proof for this leftover in famous texts. Some factors of the Prose Edda say such things as, "The earth became Odin's daughter and his accomplice," and they call Thor the god's first son. Since this tale hasn't been cautioned everywhere else, some humans assume it comes from an older tale that has been out of place: Odin married a secular goddess who moreover had a daughter or near cousin, and Thor became his heir. Scholars additionally see comparisons amongst myths as assisting this view.

A famous anthropologist thinks that Thor is like precise figures from Indo-European mythology. He says those gods are often the children of the principle god and an earth goddess. Norse writing conventions additionally seem to returned up this concept. Jord turned into as quickly as a jotunn, but the way she is indexed with the other deities is similar to how jotunnar women which incorporates Gerdr and Skadi were listed once they married into the gods. Changing ideals might also offer an cause of why Jord come to be talked about lots but did now not have any tales of her very very very own. Since Frigg have come to be Odin's companion in choice to her, Jord's testimonies might have been given to the more famous goddess. So, it is feasible that earlier than the Viking Age, people perception Odin were wed to the earth goddess in choice to Frigg. Many recollections changed her, but her name and the significance of her firstborn son stayed in Norse notion.

In Norse legend, Jord is frequently named as Thor's mom. Odin changed into his father, however no memories inform how he come to be born. Many humans name Jord a jotunn, which means "large," In the manner that female Jotunar who marry Aesir gods are typically known as goddesses, she is likewise known as certainly one of them. There are many references to Jord in myths, however none display her as a completely-formed determine. Even even though she is Thor's mother, she would possibly now not seem like with a few other gods or play each different component. But, a few students anticipate that this wasn't normally the case. In English, Jord's name method "Earth." In different Indo-European religions, leader gods and ground goddesses had been married. Her marriage to Odin and her son's importance may additionally align with this. There are recommendations within the texts which Jord can also were stable as Odin's partner inside the past. Over time, Frigg took over this position, and Jord changed into handiest referred to as the partner of 1 god without a high-quality myths linked to her.

Sol and Mani: Goddess of the Sun and Moon

They had been not like unique sky gods, regardless of the truth that; their journey across the heavens changed into to break out hungry monsters! The Norse human beings idea the goddess Sól added the sun through the sky every day. Her brother Máni went at the identical journey to the moon at night time. Both Sól and Máni went on the journey with distinctive people. Hati, a hungry wolf, become after Sól, and Skoll, Hati's sister, modified into after Máni. Both Sól and Máni were to lose their lengthy-walking race through the sky at Ragnarok.

They might be eaten through the wolves that had been after them. The manner they died at Ragnarok is a commonplace subject in Norse legend, however Sól and Máni are not sincerely Germanic characters in most unique strategies. There are many commonplace styles of sun and lunar gods that they in shape into.

The sun and moon have been represented through the gods Sól and Máni. They were siblings and the offspring of a celestial being named Mundilfari. Her sibling Máni modified into the deity of the moon, and Sól have end up the solar. Each person drew their horses across the sky with the light from their homes. There had been one of a kind humans with them, however. A giant dog became after each Sól and Máni. These had been the dogs that lived with Fenrir, Loki's monster son. They tried all day and night time time to eat Sól and Máni. Hati, the male wolf, modified into after Sól. Skoll, his sister, went after Máni further to the moon. Both sped their chariots as rapid as they could in the direction of the space to get away from the hungry wolves. Various versions of the story say that Sól, further to Máni, have been meant to mild up the arena and help humans bear in mind even as subjects occurred. At the begin of time, they did now not understand a way to get everywhere. Consequently, Odin had to show off the proper manner to move the sky.

But in a one in every of a kind story, Sól and Máni emerged as ordinary humans. Mundilfari, their father, thought they had been so pretty that he named those people after the solar and the moon. On the opposite hand, the gods were mad at what they observed due to the fact the family's delight and punished them. The children were located in the heavens to show the real sun and moon the manner. He misplaced his kids, and Sól, as well as Máni, ended up in a scenario in which they had to art work difficult and be generally careful. Hati and Skoll sped throughout the sky each day. But, like one-of-a-type gods, they knew they were doomed to lose this conflict. The puppies might in the end seize their prey at Ragnarok. Skoll and Hati would possibly seize the likes of Sól and Máni and eat them whole earlier than the very last fight.

Nothing could be visible or heard in the international. Some say that the wolves had been going to go away the earth and arrive in Midgard to devour all the useless our bodies that had been lying spherical. The Prose Edda, however, says that mild will now not be erased forever. Hati might seize Sól in reality as she changed into giving beginning to a woman. She is probably actually as quite as her mother and make it via the combat of Ragnarok. After the warfare, the gods who've been however alive might rebuild Asgard. New land may appear, and one human couple may also ascend out from the limbs of Yggdrasil. Sól's daughter ought to rise into the sky and mild up a state-of-the-art global as fast as they did.

The Norse goddess for the sun changed into Sól. The moon god have come to be her brother Máni. Each individual sped a carriage via the sky. They were being chased by a brother and sister % of wolves, who might kill them at Ragnarok. One later tale, instead, said that even after Sól similarly to Máni were killed, light might no matter the truth that be spherical. Sól's daughter might take over as sun goddess at the same time as the arena end up born over again. Ragnarok is a totally Norse story, however Sól and Máni are part of a larger sample in lots of distinct reminiscences.

In many Indo-European religions, the solar and moon are visible as separate gods, normally ladies and men. Most of the time, these celestial beings came at some point of the heavens in a few automobile. Often, they rode chariots like Sól and Máni. Also, gods were regularly referred to as the moon and the sun of their tongues. This is probably why Sól and Máni are the other genders of different gods in this faith. Because Sól and Máni are so similar to this Indo-European high-quality, they had been probable some of the number one Norse gods and function changed the least over the years.

Chapter 6: The Birth Of The Cosmos

In the dark expanse of Ginnungagap, the void that predated time and existence itself, the ancient Norse cosmology unfolds a fascinating tale of introduction and starting area. At the coronary coronary coronary heart of this cosmic narrative is Ymir, the primeval large, who emerges from the convergence of opposing forces—ice and fireplace. Ymir, neither god nor mortal however a creature of sheer chaos, turns into the genesis of the Norse universe.

Ymir's lifestyles is in detail tied to the paranormal cow Auðumbla, who sustains herself via the use of licking the salty ice of Ginnungagap. From her nourishment, Ymir attracts life, and as he slumbers, he unknowingly gives start to the primary frost giants from his left armpit and the primary gods from his proper armpit. Among those gods, Odin, the enigmatic Allfather and leader of the Aesir, takes his region as a full-size discern within the unfolding drama.

In this panorama normal by way of way of the remnants of Ymir, the gods find out themselves. Odin, alongside his brothers Vili and Ve, embark on a first rate challenge—to craft the very worldwide from Ymir's massive remains. The earth takes form from his flesh, the mountains upward push from his bones, and the boundless seas glide together together with his lifestyles's blood.

Yet, the cosmos isn't always merely a physical realm; it requires order, a framework upon which lifestyles can spread. Thus, the gods erect Yggdrasil, the superb ash tree, on the coronary coronary coronary heart of all introduction. Yggdrasil, with roots that delve deep into the Nine Realms and branches that contact the heavens, becomes the cosmic axis—the hyperlink that binds collectively each aspect of the universe. Its sprawling cover offers safe haven and colour to the area below, symbolizing the interconnections of all matters in the tough internet of Norse mythology.

The Norse idea of the cosmos, born from the frame of Ymir, customary by means of the hands of gods, and upheld by manner of the effective tree Yggdrasil, embodies a worldwide in which gods, giants, and mortals play their roles in a single, grand theater. It is a realm wherein future is etched into the very cloth of life, and wherein the play of forces, from chaos to reserve, shapes the very center of Norse mythology itself.

The Pantheon of Gods and Goddesses

Norse mythology is teeming with a severa type of gods and goddesses, every owning their very personal particular trends and roles in the cosmic drama. Here, we'll introduce you to some of the maximum top notch figures on this historical hierarchy of deities.

Odin (The Allfather)

Odin, the venerable leader of the Aesir gods, stands because the critical embodiment of data and strength inside the Norse pantheon. Often depicted as an elder deity with a distinguished beard and a singular eye, Odin's character is marked with the useful resource of his thirst for understanding. His quest for statistics led him to make a profound sacrifice, willingly relinquishing one of his eyes in alternate for the boundless insights won from the nicely of Mímir. Mímir the Wise is a lesser diagnosed God inside the Norse universe, and the Well of Mímir is a picture of the significance of know-how and sacrifice in Norse mythology.

Odin's have an effect on extends throughout a sizeable spectrum of domain names, embracing know-how, facts, poetry, warfare, and lack of existence. This eclectic collection of attributes underscores his position as a god of both creation and destruction, a divine decide who navigates the satisfactory line among order and chaos.

One of Odin's maximum notable feats is his acquisition of the runes, a mystical alphabet steeped in mystical energy. Odin's mastery of the runes reinforces his function as a multifaceted deity able to each profound perception and esoteric statistics. Read extra approximately the runes in bankruptcy 7.

Thor (The Thunder God)

Thor, the crimson-bearded and effective son of Odin, emerges as a vital and loved figure within the pantheon of Norse gods. His essence is described by using power and valor, attributes which might be vividly personified in his characteristic due to the reality the god of thunder and lightning.

Thor's most iconic possession is the legendary hammer, Mjölnir, a picture of divine energy and protection. With Mjölnir in hand, he can summon thunderstorms and wield damaging lightning bolts, correctly safeguarding the realms from the pervasive threats posed with the aid of giants, trolls, and different malevolent forces. His unwavering determination to this shielding responsibility is obvious, emphasizing his willpower to preserving order and shielding the sensitive balance of the cosmos.

Thor's exploits are not mere delusion however concrete examples of his valor. His heroic adventures and ferocious battles in competition to various adversaries, specially the giants, echo during Norse mythology. These sagas underscore his position as a guardian of Midgard, the human realm, and a paragon of bravery and resilience.

Loki (The Trickster)

Loki, the enigmatic and paradoxical figure of Norse mythology, represents a complex aggregate of developments that defies sincere elegance. His character is much like a richly woven tapestry, wherein threads of cunning and mischief intertwine, growing a multifaceted person whose moves span the spectrum from playful pranks to treacherous schemes.

At the coronary heart of Loki's essence lies his identification as a form-shifter and a trickster, attributes that function the catalysts for the discord and unpredictability that often display up inside the nation-states of each gods and mortals. Loki's capricious nature manner that his movements can range from innocent jests and realistic jokes that elicit laughter to tricky and dangerous machinations that plunge the cosmos into chaos. He embodies the archetype of the trickster, a parent determined in severa mythologies international, who stressful conditions the set up order and introduces an element of disruption and transformation.

Loki's have an effect on extends a long way past mere mischief, however. His man or woman bears a profound ambiguity this is rooted within the paradox of his moves. While Loki is regularly the instigator of strife, he is also undeniably instrumental in numerous pivotal sports inside Norse mythology. His involvement in key moments, collectively with the retrieval of treasures from the giants or his role in the start of Odin's robust steed Sleipnir, demonstrates that Loki's movements, even though disruptive, may have a long way-achieving consequences that in the long run serve the interests of the gods and the route of future.Freyja (The Goddess of Love and Fertility)

Chapter 7: The Goddess Of Love And Fertility

Freyja, a multifaceted goddess of superb beauty and attraction, occupies a outstanding characteristic in the Norse pantheon. Her area is expansive, encompassing love, fertility, beauty, and sensuality. Freyja's presence embodies the thrill and pleasures of life itself, a fascinating determine reputable thru every gods and mortals.

One of Freyja's great attributes is her twin nature. While she is extensively diagnosed for her nurturing and amorous trends, she moreover possesses formidable martial prowess. She is from time to time depicted with a cloak of falcon feathers, granting her the present of flight and underscoring her position as a warrior goddess.

Freyja shares her divine lineage collectively in conjunction with her dual brother, Freyr, who is associated with prosperity and abundance. This sibling connection highlights the importance of fertility and wealth in Norse manner of existence.

Frigg (The Queen of the Aesir)

Frigg, the companion of Odin and the matriarch of the Aesir, occupies a function of authority and maternal facts some of the gods. Her dominion centers on marriage, own family, and domesticity, emphasizing their paramount significance in Norse society.

One of Frigg's most interesting attributes is her possession of information about the future, which she guards cautiously. Her foresight performs a pivotal characteristic inside the destiny of the gods, particularly in connection to her cherished son, Baldr. Frigg's character exemplifies the maternal and nurturing factors of Norse manner of lifestyles, emphasizing the profound significance of familial bonds and the interconnections of the divine and mortal geographical regions.

Týr (The God of Law and Heroic Glory)

Týr is a god related to regulation, justice, heroic glory, and courage. He is frequently depicted as a one-exceeded god, having sacrificed his hand to bind the huge wolf Fenrir. Týr's unwavering willpower to honor and responsibility makes him a image of righteous authority and valor in Norse mythology. He is a god of justice who guarantees that oaths and agreements are upheld, embodying the mind of regulation and order.

Baldr (The God of Light and Purity)

Baldr is a radiant god associated with slight and purity. He is the son of Odin and Frigg and is understood for his superb beauty and goodness. Baldr's presence brings pride and harmony to the sector, and he's cherished by way of the usage of manner of each gods and mortals. His premature demise, because of a treacherous act, will become a essential tragedy in Norse mythology, symbolizing the fragility of innocence and goodness in a world marked thru chaos and deception. You can have a look at greater approximately Baldr's loss of existence within the paragraphs approximately the brilliant Ragnarök battles in monetary catastrophe four.

Heimdall (The Watchman of the Gods)

Heimdall is the vigilant figure of the gods and the protector of the Bifröst, the rainbow bridge that connects Asgard to Midgard. He possesses eager senses, mainly hearing, and is said to pay interest the grass develop and notice intruders from afar. Heimdall's watchful presence ensures the protection of the gods and the integrity of the Nine Realms. He is frequently depicted as a stoic and noble figure, embodying the beliefs of obligation and vigilance.

These are just a few of the gods and goddesses that populate the Norse pantheon. As we discover similarly, you'll come across more exciting figures, each with their personal memories and significance. The gods of the North are more than mere characters in a mythological tapestry; they encompass the values, virtues, and complexities of the Norse people, making them a completely crucial and critical a part of the Norse legacy.

The Nine Realms

In Norse cosmology, the universe is break up into nine geographical regions, each with its very personal top notch developments, population, and importance. These nation-states aren't isolated islands but are in element interconnected, and on the coronary heart of this cosmic net stands Yggdrasil, the splendid World Tree, which serves due to the fact the linchpin that binds the Nine Realms together.

Asgard - Realm of the Aesir Gods

Asgard, often referred to as the celestial stronghold of the Aesir gods, holds a characteristic of paramount significance inside the Norse cosmos. Situated on the zenith of the cosmic tree Yggdrasil, it exists as an ethereal and majestic realm, an extended way eliminated from the earthly aircraft of Midgard.

This celestial castle is greater than only a residing area; it represents the epicenter of divine electricity and beauty in Norse mythology. Asgard's towering spires and shimmering palaces are a testament to the opulence of the gods, reflecting their popularity as rulers of the cosmos. It is an area wherein divine authority reigns best, and the Aesir govern the destinies of mortals and the future of the world. Yet, Asgard isn't always absolutely a haven of serenity and bliss. It is a realm steeped in warfare and war, because the Aesir gods deal with the chaotic forces of the giants. These epic clashes amongst gods and giants, which incorporates the prophesied conflict of Ragnarök, play a pivotal position in Norse mythology and underline the ever-present tension among order and chaos, creation and destruction.

Asgard's significance reverberates at some stage inside the mythology, now not simply as a residing region for the gods however as a photograph of cosmic stability and divine sovereignty. It is a realm in which the forces of order and divine authority are upheld, even inside the face of coming close to near doom. As such, Asgard stands as a beacon of wish and a testomony to the long-lasting spirit of the Norse gods within the complicated and difficult tapestry of Norse mythology.

Valhalla, moreover spelled as "Valhöll" in Old Norse, is a distinguished and mythological idea in Norse mythology. It is regularly known as the "Hall of the Slain" or the "Warrior's Heaven." Valhalla is an great and massive hall located inside the realm of Asgard and is presided over thru Odin.

Valhalla serves as a totally final excursion spot for courageous and honorable warriors who die in battle. In Norse perception, warriors who fought valiantly and died with honor in combat were decided on through manner of Odin's valkyries, who were divine maidens, to be taken to Valhalla. These warriors, referred to as the Einherjar, may additionally ceremonial dinner and fight at a few degree in the day, and then their wounds may miraculously heal thru using night time, allowing them to put together for an eternal war that could take place inside the path of Ragnarök.

The idea of Valhalla turn out to be fairly esteemed in Norse way of life, because it represented a warrior's ultimate reward for valor and courage in warfare. Warriors who went to Valhalla were expected to defend the gods at a few degree inside the final warfare of Ragnarök, and their bravery in this war changed into crucial to the survival of the cosmos.

Midgard - The World of Humans

Midgard, frequently referred to as "Middle Earth" or "Middle Garden," occupies a pivotal role inside the Norse cosmos, located on the very coronary coronary heart of the Nine Realms. It is not simplest the geographical middle of the cosmos but moreover the vicinity of mortal beings, serving due to the fact the house of humanity itself. Midgard's panorama is various and fascinating, characterised through manner of way of sprawling mountains, dense forests, massive seas, and the ever-converting terrain that people name their non-public.

Within the area of Midgard, human beings thrive and face the myriad trials and tribulations of lifestyles. In the context of Norse mythology, Midgard serves as the focal point for plenty sagas and legends. It is the degree upon which heroic testimonies spread, in which courageous people challenge into the unknown, confront supernatural forces, and are looking for to go away their mark upon the sector. Midgard's testimonies are not simplest epic adventures however additionally reflections of the demanding conditions and triumphs that outline the human enjoy.

Moreover, Midgard's importance extends past its characteristic as a backdrop for myths and sagas. It embodies the interconnectedness of the Nine Realms, serving as a bridge most of the divine and the mortal. In this realm, humans navigate the complexities of existence, forging their personal paths on the equal time as every so often crossing paths with the gods and wonderful legendary beings. As a stop result, Midgard encapsulates the essence of the Norse worldview, in which the human enjoy is intimately intertwined with the divine, and in which the moves of mortals reverberate thru the entire cosmos.

Jotunheim - Land of Giants

Jotunheim, sometimes referred to as Jotunheimr or Jotunheimen in Old Norse, is a realm shrouded in fantasy and thriller, domestic to the bold beings called Jotnar, or giants. Jotunheim stands as a realm of stark assessment to the celestial splendor of Asgard and the human international of Midgard. It is an area wherein primal forces and chaotic energies hold sway, and the boundaries amongst order and chaos blur proper into a realm of perpetual tension.

Inhabitants of Jotunheim, the Jotnar, are beings of large stature and great power, frequently depicted as competition and adversaries to the Aesir gods, which includes Odin, Thor, and Freyja. Their interactions with the gods are marked by using manner of a normal situation of war, symbolizing the everlasting war amongst divine authority and unruly, untamed forces. Giants embody the uncooked, untamed factors of nature and lifestyles, making Jotunheim a realm of unpredictability and danger.

Notably, figures like Loki, hail from Jotunheim, along with layers of complexity to the realm. Loki's twin nature as every a mischief-maker and an occasional exceptional buddy exemplifies the multifaceted man or woman of Jotunheim. It is an area wherein alliances may be as fickle due to the fact the winds that sweep during its rugged landscapes, supplying every perilous demanding situations and capability opportunities for individuals who dare to venture inner.

It's well well worth noting that Jotunheim additionally holds a real-worldwide counterpart in the form of a National Park positioned in Norway. This earthly realm, which shares its call with the mythological land of giants, is a place of breathtaking natural splendor, with massive mountain levels, glaciers, and pristine wasteland. While the National Park bears no direct connection to the mythological Jotunheim, it serves as a testomony to the iconic have an impact on of Norse mythology on the cultural and geographical landscape of the place.

Vanaheim - Home of the Vanir Gods

Vanaheim is a realm inhabited via the Vanir gods, a set of deities associated with fertility, prosperity, and nature. It is a lush and colorful land, contrasting with the sternness of Asgard. The Vanir and the Aesir engaged in a superb struggle in the beyond, but they in the long run exchanged hostages, fostering peace and cooperation.

Alfheim - Realm of the Light Elves

Alfheim is home to the airy moderate elves, beings identified for their splendor and charm. While it's miles one of the lesser-explored geographical areas in Norse mythology, it's miles an area of enchantment and thriller, frequently associated with light and purity.

Svartalfheim - Domain of the Dark Elves (Dwarves)

Svartalfheim is inhabited through the darkish elves, typically called dwarves. These expert craftsmen are stated for their mastery of metalwork and magic. Svartalfheim is in which the famous sons of Ivaldi, expert artisans, create powerful artifacts.

Helheim - Realm of the Dead

Helheim is a realm related to the useless, presided over through the use of the use of the goddess Hel. It is an area in which souls skip after death, and it's miles divided into sections for the virtuous, the wicked, and people who die of vintage age or infection.

Niflheim - Land of Ice and Mist

Niflheim is a realm of freezing cold and everlasting mist. It is the birthplace of ice and contrasts with the fiery Muspelheim. Niflheim is frequently associated with the primordial being Ymir and the appearance of the cosmos.

Muspelheim - Land of Fire

Muspelheim is a realm of hearth and heat, dominated through the hearth large Surtr. It stands in opposition to the icy Niflheim, and together, they contributed to the arrival of the cosmos. Muspelheim represents chaos and negative forces.

These Nine Realms shape the inspiration of Norse cosmology, every presenting its non-public disturbing situations, wonders, and narratives.

Chapter 8: The Twilight Of The Gods

At the coronary coronary heart of Norse mythology lies a haunting and cataclysmic prophecy—a vision of a international devastation called Ragnarök. This financial ruin dives deep into the chilling narrative of an apocalyptic end that has left a mark on Norse manner of existence and imagination. Ragnarök, which translates to "Fate of the Gods" or "Twilight of the Gods," is a chain of interconnected activities that mark the area's lack of lifestyles and the dawning of a modern-day day generation.

The saga of Ragnarök starts offevolved with the chilling arrival of the Fimbulwinter, an unrelenting and brutal wintry weather that spans three harrowing years. During this frigid length, the world is plunged into an abyss of darkness and biting bloodless. It is a time of profound chaos and struggling, wherein the very fabric of society is torn asunder, and ethical values erode underneath the weight of despair.

As the Fimbulwinter blankets the cosmos in icy depression, ominous symptoms and signs and symptoms and symptoms and portents start to emerge. Wolves voraciously devour the solar and the moon, casting the sector into perpetual darkness. The stars vanish from the night time time sky, and the earth shudders and quakes underneath the upcoming shadow of doom.

The pivotal 2d arrives with the resounding blast of Gjallarhorn, the cosmic horn sounded thru Heimdall, the vigilant figure of the gods. Its mournful name reverberates all through the Nine Realms, serving as both an ominous deliver in and a rallying cry to the gods, summoning them to put together for the final reckoning.

In the face of this looming disaster, the gods collect their forces to confront the relentless tide of chaos and destruction. Among the epic battles that transpire, one of the maximum massive is the Battle of Ragnarök—a big conflict many of the Aesir gods and the Jotnar, the giants. It is a battle that wishes a devastating toll, claiming the lives of gods and giants alike, and culminating in the fiery conflagration that consumes the area itself.

Within the complex tale of Ragnarök's grim narrative, the destruction isn't always entirely restrained to the battlefield clashes; it extends to encompass a series of pivotal activities that collectively supply inside the world's inexorable descent into chaos and devastation.

The first of these somber episodes centers round Baldr, the cherished god of slight and purity. Baldr's tragic lack of life, marked thru a treacherous arrow, serves as a poignant second that resonates at some stage in the cosmos. His loss of life is not most effective a loss of a cherished deity but a symbolic harbinger, signaling the commencement of Ragnarök—a global-changing occasion with a purpose to see the very foundations of life disintegrate.

Amidst the chaos, the giant wolf Fenrir, a effective pressure lengthy certain in chains via the gods, in the long run breaks free from his fetters. This momentous occasion unfolds within the tumultuous theater of the very last conflict, because the outstanding wolf unleashes his wrath upon the divine pantheon. In a chilling climax, Odin, the respectable Allfather and leader of the Aesir, will become Fenrir's tragic prey, devoured inside the chaos of Ragnarök. Odin's loss of lifestyles represents a profound turning factor, signifying the ultimate vulnerability of even the mightiest of gods.

Simultaneously, the depths of the sea yield a malevolent strain of notable importance— the Midgard Serpent, Jormungandr. Rising from its aquatic abode, this huge serpent heralds torrents of floods and cataclysmic chaos that inundate the location, in addition intensifying the relentless destruction. Its emergence underscores the overpowering and uncontrollable forces which is probably let loose upon the cosmos in the route of Ragnarök.

These activities, on the equal time as in my view tragic and catastrophic, are inseparably intertwined, collectively shaping the apocalyptic narrative of Ragnarök. Baldr's loss of lifestyles marks the prelude, Odin's fall symbolizes the vulnerability of divine beings, Fenrir's liberation embodies the untamable power of chaos, and Jormungandr's emergence from the depths exemplifies the tide of destruction that sweeps all through the cosmos. Together, they make a contribution to the profound enjoy of doom and finality that permeates the coronary coronary heart-wrenching saga of the Twilight of the Gods.

As the cataclysmic battles rage on, the very material of the cosmos starts offevolved to solve. The international is consumed via flames, the sky darkens, and the earth is submerged underneath the turbulent seas.

The gods and giants, locked in a brutal battle, meet their inescapable destinies.

However, from the ashes of this devastation arises the promise of renewal. The prevent of Ragnarök heralds the rebirth of the place—a modern and fertile earth emerges from the waters, teeming with capacity and preference. Surviving gods and those, rising from their sanctuaries, embark on the adventure to repopulate the sector. The rebirth of Baldr and Höðr, the god of darkness, symbolizes the cyclical nature of life, wherein lifestyles and desire bear even inside the face of overwhelming destruction.

Ragnarök, in all its profundity and solemnity, serves as a poignant mirrored photo of the Norse worldview—a cosmos woven with threads of advent and destruction, in which cycles of life and demise are inextricably related. It stands as a stark reminder that, even in the darkest hour of calamity, there is the iconic capability for renewal and the undying flame of wish.

Heroic Sagas and Legends

Within the rich records of Norse mythology, a treasure of epic sagas and mythical tales awaits discovery. These sagas are extra than mere reminiscences; they will be the iconic echoes of data, the chronicles of honor, and the embodiment of the unyielding human spirit. As we delve into this financial catastrophe, we're able to now not exceptional find out the riveting narratives but additionally find out the essence of what makes a saga in truth great.

But earlier than we retain, it's critical to make easy what exactly a "saga" represents within the context of Norse literature. In Old Norse, the time period "saga" refers to a story or story, often recounting the deeds and adventures of heroes, warriors, and tremendous figures. These sagas feature a bridge among records and fantasy, presenting insights into the lives, values, and struggles of the humans of the Viking Age. They are memories of valor, tragedy, and the inexhaustible human spirit, surpassed down through generations as a testament to the long-lasting legacy of the Norse international.

Sigurd and the Dragon (Volsunga Saga)

The saga of Sigurd, additionally called the Volsunga Saga, is a cornerstone of Norse literature. It tells the story of Sigurd the Dragon Slayer, who embarks on a quest to rescue a cursed princess and slay the robust dragon Fafnir. This saga is complete of topics of heroism, betrayal, and the effects of greed. Sigurd's valor and tragic destiny have made him an extended lasting image of heroism in Norse way of life.

Beowulf

While not a strictly Norse saga, the epic poem "Beowulf" is a masterpiece of Old English literature with sturdy Norse affects.

It recounts the exploits of Beowulf, a Geatish warrior, as he battles the massive Grendel, the ocean hag, and a fearsome dragon. The poem displays difficulty topics of heroism, loyalty, and the eternal struggle among proper and evil, and it has had a profound effect on medieval literature.

The Valkyries

The Valkyries are effective woman figures in Norse mythology, tasked with choosing fallen warriors to accompany them to Valhalla, Odin's excellent hall in Asgard. Their role in deciding on the bravest and maximum honorable warriors has made them iconic figures in Norse life-style. The idea of the Valkyries has moreover found its manner into present day interpretations of Norse mythology, shaping the portrayal of fierce, warrior girls.

The Saga of the Ynglings (Ynglinga Saga)

The Saga of the Ynglings, referred to as the Ynglinga Saga, is a fascinating narrative that serves as a historical tapestry tracing the lineage of the illustrious Yngling dynasty. According to their proud data, they'll be believed to be direct descendants of the god Frey, a deity carefully associated with fertility, prosperity, and the bounties of nature.

The Ynglinga Saga does greater than truly gift a own family tree; it weaves collectively the threads of an epic tapestry that showcases the heroic exploits and legendary deeds of these Norse monarchs. With each flip of the net web page, readers are transported right into a international wherein valor and courage are celebrated, wherein kings upward push to the event to protect their geographical areas, and in which the echoes in their deeds reverberate via the a long term. This saga becomes a residing testament to the indomitable spirit of the Yngling dynasty, leaving an indelible mark at the information of the Norse human beings.

Hrolf Kraki's Saga

This saga tells the story of Hrolf Kraki, a legendary Danish king and warrior. His battles towards supernatural foes, along with the big troll Grendel, showcase his valor and prowess. The saga explores subjects of bravery, honor, and the supernatural, leaving an indelible mark on Norse literature.

These sagas and legends are not satisfactory charming stories of heroism and adventure but also domestic home windows into the values and beliefs of the Norse humans. They replicate the importance of honor, courage, and loyalty in Norse subculture, and their enduring have an effect on may be visible in later literature, artwork, and present day famous manner of life.

The Birth of Edda

The Edda holds a very precise and respected reputation within the realm of Norse literature. It is not simply a set of narratives or heroic memories; as a substitute, it's far a compendium of facts, a repository of the understanding, poetry, and cosmology of the historic North. In its pages, we find out the keys to statistics the complex internet of Norse ideals, the complexities in their poetic traditions, and the underlying structure of their mythological international.

But what sets the Edda other than unique sagas is its origins. It became no longer born out of the need to chronicle the deeds of kings or heroes, nor does it recount the sagas of man or woman figures. Instead, it's miles the product of a aware attempt to hold and transmit the cultural historic past of the Norse humans. The Edda modified into crafted as a compendium of poetic and mythological understanding, lovingly assembled via pupils and poets who diagnosed the want to shield the essence in their way of life for future generations.

The Origins of the Edda

The origins of the Edda may be traced once more to the rugged and a long manner off terrain of medieval Iceland, a land described by way of its untamed barren location, harsh weather, and a stark, setting apart splendor. This geographically secluded society, located on the brink of the regarded worldwide, served as a crucible wherein a first rate literary masterpiece modified into forged—a testament to human ingenuity and determination inside the presence of daunting adversities.

In this remoted context, storytelling have become no longer in reality a hobby however an intrinsic part of life itself. The lengthy, dark winters and the seclusion imposed thru Iceland's geography created an surroundings in which the spoken and sung word took on a profound importance. Within the walls of humble farmsteads and amidst the essential forces of nature, narratives had been spun like golden threads, connecting generations to the ancestral past.

It is interior this crucible of ice and fireplace that the Edda emerged as a notable testament to the tenacity and cultural devotion of its nameless poets. These poets had been now not mere scribes; they have been torchbearers of a manner of life that stretched lower back in time immemorial. They navigated the treacherous waters of linguistic evolution, preserving and reshaping historical recollections in verse and prose, making sure that the collective reminiscence of the Norse people remained vibrant and intact.

The Edda, as an entire, is a multifaceted treasure comprising critical elements—the Poetic Edda and the Prose Edda. These components provide wonderful lenses thru which we will view Norse mythology, every contributing uniquely to our knowledge.

Chapter 9: The Poetic Tradition

The Poetic Edda, a set of historical poems, acts as a bridge to the past. These poetic compositions function time tablets, retaining the voices and visions of generations of skalds—gifted storytellers in their time. These verses not tremendous offer narratives of delusion however additionally encapsulate the ethical ideals of honor, permitting us to find out the cultural ethos of the technology.

In Norse lifestyle, poetry held a function of paramount significance, transcending mere enjoyment. It changed into a respected manner of maintaining information, myth, and the ethical values of honor and bravery. Skaldic poetry, with its tough paperwork and systems, have become a repository of ancient expertise, weaving the memories of gods and heroes proper right into a wealthy tapestry. These poetic compositions had been no longer useless recitations however dwelling expressions of a culture deeply entwined with its mythology. They embodied the spirit of a human beings whose reverence for his or her ancient beyond knew no bounds.

The Prose Tradition

On the opposite, the Prose Edda, attributed to Snorri Sturluson, functions as a literary guide, providing precious insights into the mechanics of Norse myths. Snorri's paintings no longer most effective serves as a protection vessel for these myths but moreover extensively affects how we understand and interact with them in the context of our modern-day-day global. By illuminating the artwork of storytelling, the Prose Edda acts as a essential bridge across the chasm of centuries, rendering the historic myths available and continuously relevant.

Within the Prose Edda, Snorri Sturluson's narrative brilliance takes center diploma. This masterpiece not only retells the myths however moreover affords a established framework for their interpretation and appreciation. Snorri's skillful storytelling ensures that those age-antique myths go beyond the bounds of time, shaping our current expertise of Norse mythology. The Prose Edda, in essence, stands as an act of cultural guardianship, making sure that the enduring myths it safeguards stay colourful and charming for generations to return.

The Significance Today

Even in our cutting-edge international, the Edda maintains to weave its attraction, charming students, writers, artists, and fanatics throughout the globe. Its tales are complete of essential mind like heroes, destiny, and the connection amongst gods and ordinary human beings. These memories are like a replicate that shows us components of what it technique to be human, and that's why they'll be crucial to human beings from unique times and locations. The Edda maintains the Norse myths alive and facilitates them live vital in our changing international.

8 Runes and Symbols

The runic alphabet stands as a radiant thread in Norse Mythology, weaving its manner thru the very cloth of their civilization. Its presence is not certainly symbolic; it is a living testament to the profound significance that runes held—a repository of ancient data, a device for conversation, divination, and a conduit for magical practices.

At its middle, runes had been a realistic technique of communication. In a society wherein the written word turned into now not as regular as it's miles in recent times, runes served as a device for recording records, conveying messages, and staining ownership. They embellished the whole thing from runestones that memorialized the deeds of heroes to everyday gadgets like rings, amulets, and weapons, imbuing the ones gadgets with a hint of the mystical and the sacred.

Yet, the vicinity of runes extended a long way past the mundane. They were in element entwined with the non secular and the magical additives of Norse culture. The runic script changed into believed to be a present from the god Odin himself, who, in a legendary sacrifice, hung from the World Tree, Yggdrasil, for nine days and nights to build up the understanding of the runes. This divine beginning infused the runes with a sense of magic and thriller, making them a effective medium for divination and spellcasting.

In the palms of runemasters and seers, runes had been used to looking for steering from the spirit international, to anticipate the destiny, and to launch the hidden truths of lifestyles. Casting runes modified right into a solemn ritual, and the results had been interpreted with reverence and awe, for they had been believed to reveal the selection of the gods and the forces shaping the lives of mortals.

The Runic Alphabet

The Runic Alphabet is likewise known as the Futhark, and is a completely unique writing tool that boasts a hard and fast of angular characters, each symbolizing a superb sound, and it held a profound importance within the lives of the Norse people.

Carved into stone, etched onto wood, and inscribed onto historic artifacts, runes have been now not actually characters; they had been providers of a non secular and cultural historical past. Each rune possessed its personal unique shape, call, and related which means, and together they shaped a device that encapsulated the records, beliefs, and evaluations of the Norse human beings.

The Futhark's origins may be traced to the early Germanic tribes, and it underwent numerous variations as it journeyed via time and throughout the expanse of the Northern lands. Indeed, the runic alphabet have come to be more than just a tool for recording phrases; it changed into a residing, breathing testomony to the language, subculture, and spirituality of the Norse humans. It carried with it the burden of way of life, the strength of verbal exchange, and the essence of a civilization deeply rooted in its roots and looking closer to the future with an unwavering connection to the beyond.

Writing with Runes

The act of writing with runes transcended the conventional barriers of linguistic expression; it modified right into a cultural and creative undertaking that left a mark at the fabric and spiritual international of the Norse human beings.

Yet, runes have been not limited to public monuments and epic tales by myself. They positioned their way into the most intimate factors of Norse lifestyles. Personal messages, etched onto amulets and tokens, carried expressions of love, safety, and wish. These runic inscriptions, infused with personal sentiment, have turn out to be loved possessions, guardians of secrets and techniques, and assets of solace in an unpredictable global.

Writing with runes come to be greater than a beneficial act; it have become an creative project, a manner of carving the essence of the Norse spirit into the very material of their life. Runes transcended the written phrase; they had been residing expressions of a manner of life deeply related to its language, its memories, and its human beings.

Chapter 10: Norse Mythology In Modern Film & Tv-Shows

In the arena of modern-day-day leisure, the echoes of Norse mythology resound loudly, transcending the annals of statistics to find a new domestic in television video display units throughout the globe. The enchantment of the Norse cosmos, with its famous gods, epic battles, and wealthy storytelling, has left an indelible mark on modern film and TV shows and has emerge as a wellspring of notion for issues, characters, and tale strains.

Thor (2011) - "Thor" is a Marvel superhero movie that brings the Norse God of Thunder, Thor, to existence. Drawing intently from Norse mythology, it explores the adventure of Thor, the crown prince of Asgard, as he is exiled to Earth and want to prove himself worth of his powers and the throne. The movie showcases the legendary realm of Asgard, the hammer-wielding

Mjölnir, and different factors rooted in Norse mythology.

Thor: The Dark World (2013) - In this sequel to an appropriate Thor film, the darkish elf Malekith threatens to plunge the universe into darkness the use of a powerful historic artifact referred to as the Aether. Thor need to once more name upon his godly powers to protect every Earth and the Nine Realms.

Thor: Ragnarok (2017) - The 0.33 Thor movie explores the concept of Ragnarök, the prophesied surrender of the area in Norse mythology. It takes a funny method on the equal time as however delving into the apocalyptic issues and characters from Norse legends.

Valhalla Rising (2009) - Directed with the useful aid of Nicolas Winding Refn, this surreal and atmospheric movie is ready in Viking instances and explores mission matters of destiny, violence, and spirituality. It draws idea from Norse mythology in its portrayal of a one-eyed warrior and the search for because of this.

Beowulf (2007) - While no longer absolutely Norse, this change of the Old English epic poem "Beowulf" features elements from Germanic and Norse legends. It includes epic battles with legendary creatures like Grendel and a dragon.

"Vikings" (2013-2020) stands as a substantial historic drama collection that has left an indelible mark at the portrayal of Norse facts and mythology on television. Set in opposition to the backdrop of the Viking Age, the display follows the mythical Viking chieftain Ragnar Lothbrok and his descendants as they embark on epic trips of exploration, raiding, and agreement throughout the recognised international.

What devices "Vikings" aside is its functionality to seamlessly combination severa elements of Norse myths, gods, and cultural traditions into its narrative tapestry.

It brings the Viking Age to life with meticulous interest to element, from the intricacies of Viking ships to the rites and rituals that defined their way of life. While the collection captures the essence of the era and certain historic sports, it also takes revolutionary liberties to craft a compelling and dramatic storyline.

Characters like Ragnar Lothbrok and his sons are stimulated by means of using way of legendary figures from Norse sagas and chronicles, permitting viewers to connect to the ones massive-than-life heroes and anti-heroes. The collection masterfully intertwines ancient activities with mythical elements, growing a in truth immersive viewing experience in which gods and mortals coexist inside the same worldwide. This fusion of facts and mythology serves to move audiences lower again in time to an age of exploration, conquest, and cultural change, all whilst fueling their creativeness with the long-lasting appeal of Norse legends.

As the characters in "Vikings" navigate their journeys of conquest and discovery, moreover they confront the complexities in their ideals and the have an effect on of gods and fate on their lives. This dynamic exploration of religion and mythology offers intensity to the characters and their quests, highlighting the ever-gift tension a number of the mortal realm and the divine. In doing so, "Vikings" now not nice entertains however additionally invitations viewers to contemplate the significance of mythology and perception structures in shaping the direction of records—a testament to the iconic strength of Norse myths in modern-day storytelling.

"The Almighty Johnsons" (2011-2013) is a captivating New Zealand TV collection that playfully reimagines Norse mythology in a modern-day context. At its coronary coronary heart, the show revolves round a family of reincarnated Norse gods who discover themselves dwelling in contemporary New Zealand. Each member of the family inherits unique powers mirroring their divine contrary numbers from Norse mythology.

What gadgets "The Almighty Johnsons" apart is its departure from ancient or mythological accuracy. Instead, it takes a lighthearted and inventive approach to how ancient gods would likely navigate the modern-day-day international. Through humor, the collection explores time-honored topics inclusive of own family and identification, all while reflecting on how historical beliefs maintain to persuade our lives within the contemporary worldwide. This progressive fusion of Norse mythology with contemporary comedy offers a sparkling perspective on the enduring relevance of historical legends.

"American Gods" (2017-2021) is a groundbreaking TV collection tailored from

Neil Gaiman's celebrated novel, and it boldly reimagines the coexistence of historic gods and mythological beings in contemporary-day America. The show introduces visitors to a charming array of deities from a massive amount of mythologies, with tremendous appearances thru Norse gods together with Odin, who assumes a critical position inside the narrative.

At its center, "American Gods" is a idea-frightening exploration of ways those age-vintage divine entities grapple with the complexities of relevance and electricity in a worldwide that is swiftly evolving and dropping its vintage beliefs. The series refrains from adhering strictly to historic or mythological accuracy, opting instead for a daring and ingenious technique to portraying mythological figures as they adapt to trendy society.

"American Gods" immerses its target marketplace in a rich tapestry of cultures, myths, and ideals, tough conventional notions of spirituality and the supernatural. It offers a captivating exploration of the complicated relationship among gods and mortals, belief and disbelief, all within the backdrop of a current-day America in which the bounds among truth and mythology blur.

"The Last Kingdom" (2015-2021) is a gripping historical drama collection that transports web page site visitors decrease again to the Viking Age, immersing them inside the tumultuous struggle among the Saxons and Vikings in England. While the gathering in popular specializes in historical activities and political intrigue, it subtly weaves elements of Norse lifestyle, rituals, and notion systems into the cloth of its storytelling.

Unlike some precise TV shows that prominently function Norse mythology, "The Last Kingdom" does now not foreground those mythological elements.

Instead, it gives a nuanced angle on the lives of Viking characters and their interactions with the Saxons, presenting a glimpse into the cultural intricacies of the time.

One of the standout skills of "The Last Kingdom" is its determination to historic accuracy in phrases of activities, cultures, and battles. The series is going to top notch lengths to painting the Viking presence in England authentically, taking photographs the complexities in their society, which includes their customs, non secular practices, and social systems. This dedication to historic realism allows website visitors to benefit a deeper know-how of the Viking way of lifestyles and their interactions with the encircling international.

"Valhalla" (2022-) emerges as a exciting Netflix collection that transports audiences to the heart of the Viking Age, in which history and mythology intertwine to form a spell binding narrative. This series takes perception from the wealthy tapestry of Norse legends but also dares to forge its very personal path, embracing progressive liberties to craft a totally specific and unique tale.

"Valhalla" delves right proper right into a tapestry of issues that outline the Viking ethos—honor, battle, and mythology. It follows a hard and fast of valiant warriors, each with their non-public motivations and aspirations, as they navigate the treacherous landscapes in their time. This exploration of honor and warfare within a mythological framework provides intensity to the characters and their quests, imparting a nuanced portrayal of the human situation amidst the backdrop of Norse mythology.

The collection offers an interesting and visually fascinating revel in, inviting visitors to discover the arena of Norse mythology inside a fictionalized context. As they witness the exploits of these warriors and their encounters with mythical beings, visitors are treated to an interesting combination of movement, drama, and folklore.

In essence, "Valhalla" gives a sparkling and creative tackle the enduring appeal of Norse mythology, showcasing the techniques wherein ancient legends maintain to captivate contemporary audiences. It serves as a testomony to the enduring fascination with the Viking Age and the undying appeal of the mythical geographical areas that hold to shape our expertise of information and storytelling.

Chapter 11: Viking Age

Commencing within the mid-7th century and concluding throughout the year 1100, the Viking Age unfolds out over 3 centuries. During this period, the Vikings, infamous for pillaging settlements and expanding territories, ventured into uncharted territories. Despite prevailing stereotypes, which include horned battle helmets and imposing facial hair, the real individual of the Vikings stays elusive, with little firsthand documentation in their beyond.

The Vikings exhibited little hobby in documenting their facts, resulting in a lack of firsthand payments The splendid distances among Viking organizations similarly restrained the preservation in their records, leaving us with statistics in massive element sourced from their adversaries or composed prolonged after their disappearance.

The Vikings, originating from Scandinavia, have been prolific raiders and explorers who traversed the globe. Their forays into unexpected regions marked them due to the fact the first Europeans to attack and discover territories as diverse because of the reality the Middle East, Africa, and North America.

Many pinpoint the graduation of the Viking Age to the Lindisfarne attack in 792, in which Vikings focused a Christian monastery. This occasion, a catalyst for the improvement of Viking way of lifestyles, intensified Christian disdain for the ones polytheistic heathens.

Over the following centuries, Viking records spread out as a continuing collection of raids and explorations. The death of their technology, considering the quantity in their journeys, becomes much less sudden. Various theories try and provide an explanation for the using strain at the back of Viking global exploration, alongside side the choice to avoid conversion by manner of Charlemagne for the duration of the Saxon

Wars and the exercise of granting newly acquired land to the eldest son, doubtlessly motivating more more youthful sons to are looking for for wealth independently.

The Vikings' desired mode of transportation, the longship, completed a pivotal role of their worldwide have an impact on. Recognized for their adaptability, those ships, geared up with each oars and sails, allowed the Vikings to navigate various waters and come to be the number one Europeans to go the Atlantic Ocean with the resource of centuries.

The Vikings, credited with sizable discoveries, along side Greenland, attributed to Erik the Red, and North America, settled with the resource of Leif Erikson. Despite their accomplishments, the Vikings skilled losses in territory and conversions to Christianity over the years.

After assuring the French monarch of his conversion to Christianity and the exclusion of various Vikings from controlled Normandy, the Viking chief Rollo end up granted kingship, symbolizing a shift inside the Viking narrative.

Trade and Travel

The graduation of the Viking Age is typically associated with the notorious raid on Lindisfarne Monastery. Nevertheless, a dissenting view posits an earlier inception, contending that the Viking Age initiated seventy years before their Lindisfarne invasion. This predates their infamous stumble upon with the Danes on the equal time as Vikings sailed from Norway to a change port on Denmark's coast.

The Vikings, upon setting up touch with the Danes, transitioned from conventional trade to a more formalized trade channel. Archaeological discoveries of reindeer antler combs in Denmark bolster the hypothesis of this buying and selling path. Carbon courting locations the starting area of these combs to the 12 months 720 AD, and their presence in Denmark shows a alternate hyperlink between the two regions.

Contrary to the belief of Vikings as opportunistic raiders, those findings task the notion, highlighting a duration of change that normal them as expert seafarers. The Vikings' reliance on reindeer antlers shows a practical alternate in preference to mere plunder, laying the muse for his or her later maritime exploits.

Women During Vikings Age

In the Age of the Vikings, every ladies and men ventured collectively on their travels. Previously, the prevailing belief have become that Vikings, upon attaining new territories, may indiscriminately seize some thing they desired, such as girls. This belief modified in 2014 on the same time as DNA information revealed that Viking guys often journeyed with female companions to locations like Canada and Russia, even participating in expeditions to assist populate new territories.

The presence of woman Vikings accomplished a essential characteristic in the colonization of Iceland. Contrary to the idea that Vikings recruited girls domestically on the equal time as putting in place new cities, it have turn out to be the female Vikings who contributed to the agreement of Iceland. Responsible for tending to plants inside the absence of guys within the direction of raids or deaths, they executed a critical characteristic in maintaining companies.

Feasts During Vikings Age

Renowned for their prowess as raiders and sailors, the Vikings have been further famed for his or her extravagant feasts. Hosts sought to show off their wealth and authority by using using using internet web hosting lavish dinners, in which beer and steak were massive. These feasts served political purposes, fostering alliances and garnering the want of nearby agencies.

Feasts were extra regular than inner strife among numerous Viking agencies, suggesting a desire for conviviality over struggle. However, this technique confronted disturbing situations in Iceland because of a surprising ice age, prolonging winters to nine months. The extreme cold constrained cows interior, restricting grazing, and forcing Vikings to depend upon saved additives.

To cope with the unfavorable situations, the Vikings of Iceland shifted their reputation to sheep herding, higher appropriate to the tough climate. The ice age additionally wiped out the leader locations of authority for the Danes, as pondered in Viking sagas in which they ceased to be referred to. Deprived of beer and food services, the as quickly as-well-known chiefs out of place their following, emphasizing the cultural importance of feasts in Viking society.

Drug Usage

In Old Norse literature, a unusual u . S . A . Termed "berserker," loosely translated as "undergo pictures," is described. Viking warriors, reaching a trance-like scenario of anger, might also have precipitated this state via the consumption of Amanita muscaria, a hallucinogenic mushroom. The American Journal of Psychiatry proposed in 1956 that Vikings ingested those mushrooms ritually earlier than undertaking violent conflicts.

Descriptions of the berserker united states of america align with the results of mushroom intake, and archaeological evidence helps the presence of these mushrooms in Scandinavia at some diploma inside the Viking Age. Cautionary recommendation emerges: if furnished mushrooms with the resource of someone of Viking ancestry, a polite decline may be so as.

Chapter 12: Teeth Alteration Among Vikings

Historical data verify that Vikings indeed filed their tooth. An anthropological take a look at thru a Swedish researcher located out that 24 out of 557 Viking skeletons (circa 850-1050 AD) exhibited horizontally filed the front tooth, growing uniform top. The purpose and technique of this dental alteration stay unknown.

Speculation arises concerning the begin of this exercising, suggesting West Africans can also have stimulated the Vikings, even though West Africans customary teeth into factors in place of submitting them horizontally. The fearsome look, important to Viking war processes, might also have precipitated this dental alteration. Notably, the simplest appeared parallel dental submitting is amongst Native Americans within the Great Lakes location, raising the possibility of Viking interaction all through their quick presence in Newfoundland, Canada.

Mastery of the Water

The Vikings' unprecedented mastery of the seas stands out as a remarkable fulfillment. Originating from Scandinavia, they explored and traversed extra of the globe than any contemporaneous way of life. Notably, they reached current-day-day Russia and North America, settling there 500 years before Christopher Columbus.

Their amazing capability to cowl giant distances became attributed to compass generation, putting them apart from one-of-a-kind cultures in their time. While sunlight hours sailing counting on solar monitoring turned into commonplace, the Vikings' advanced compass allowed middle of the night and cloudy climate navigation. Despite the shortage of 11th-century compass fragments, a discovery in Greenland pointers at a wood disk likely used alongside flat hardwood slabs and sunstone crystals, showcasing the advanced navigational equipment hired through way of using the Vikings.

A Source of Strength and Health

In Norse mythology, the younger Odin purportedly acquired energy through the intake of mead, a beverage pretty esteemed with the beneficial aid of the Vikings. Legends additionally stated fallen warriors being bestowed with a cup of mead in Valhalla, their paradise. Far from being a legendary elixir, mead have grow to be a tangible concoction that done a exquisite function within the Vikings' lives.

Central to mead's composition become honey, a herbal substance appeared for its antibacterial and regenerative homes. The Vikings, through incorporating mead into their healthy dietweight-reduction plan, harnessed the fitness blessings of honey. During the fermentation technique, the lactic acid micro organism in honey advanced, resulting in a great boom from 1 billion to one hundred billion in line with gram. This transformation endowed mead with antibacterial homes, bolstering the Vikings' properly-being and fortifying them in opposition to ailments.

Unraveling Complex Relations

Contrary to the belief of animosity, historical evidence suggests a complex courting amongst Vikings and Christians. While Vikings frequently raided Christian institutions, specifically church homes and monasteries, it changed into not normally an expression of hostility toward Christianity. Rather, the Vikings' polytheistic ideals and openness to diverse deities contributed to their interactions with the Christian God.

The preference of non secular systems as raid targets may moreover had been pragmatic, pushed through the attraction of valuables and lax safety. Beyond encounters with Christians, the Vikings ventured as some distance due to the truth the Middle East, putting in a trade path with Persia a millennium in the beyond. This remarkable connection surfaced at the same time as the two civilizations crossed paths at the Russian steppes.

Viking Ventures

The Vikings, acknowledged for their seafaring prowess, prolonged their advantage to the Middle East, sporting out trade and exploration. A top notch item they acquired end up Persian silk, a highly-priced correct that held importance. Evidence of this modification emerged from the excavation of a burial ship in Norway relationship decrease again to 834 AD, which contained Persian silk. Intriguingly, a statue corresponding to a sitting Buddha changed into moreover positioned on the deliver, raising questions about capability touch with Buddhist cultures.

Beyond their exploits in faraway lands, the Vikings left an indelible mark on Ireland. Cities like Dublin have been based thru those seafaring people, shaping the cultural and ancient panorama of the place.

The residence mouse, scientifically known as Mus musculus domesticus, has mounted its presence on every continent except Antarctica. Intriguingly, the Vikings performed an inadvertent position in the worldwide distribution of those creatures, particularly in Europe.

It is appreciably believed that residence mice have emerge as huge, specially in Europe, with the aid of using hitching rides on Norse Viking ships. The Vikings unwittingly served as tremendous tour partners for mice, offering them with a way to disperse during uncharted territories. Concealing within the food materials crucial for Viking expeditions, mice need to with out troubles infiltrate the walls of Viking systems.

Researchers carried out a genetic test and own family tree introduction, revealing the difficult connection among Viking sports activities activities and the proliferation of residence mice. The ancestry of these rodents modified into traced, showcasing a wonderful boom in the mouse populace in Europe concurrent with the Vikings' expansive travels. Whether the Vikings were privy to the mouse infestation remains a thriller, in spite of the fact that historic evaluations advise the transportation of felines thru the Vikings.

From the 8th century AD onward, a tough and rapid of people emerged from the Scandinavian peninsula, all of the time etching their location in statistics because the Vikings. This ambitious collective of raiders, shoppers, and explorers released right into a journey of growth in the course of the diagnosed international.

The Vikings' exploits extended a ways beyond their Scandinavian origins, as they ventured to severa areas, leaving an indelible mark on information. Notable some of the locations visited and pillaged had been Russia, the Byzantine Empire, and the territories to the west and north.

In northern Scotland, a tough and speedy of settlers made a giant impact as they first arrived and mounted themselves at the islands of Shetland and Orkney. Their journey endured as they ventured to the uninhabited Faroe Islands, placed halfway amongst Scotland and Iceland. The Norsemen, pioneers of exploration, sailed to those islands, marking the primary human presence on the land about 60 years later.

Icelandic Conquest and Greenland Discovery

As data spread out, northern sailors positioned the plentiful fishing and whaling grounds in the Atlantic, main to the reputation quo of Iceland as their home base. Notably, the primary European to glimpse Greenland come to be a Norwegian sailor named Gunnbjorn Ulfsson.

Subsequently, Leif Ericson, discovered with the aid of settlers from Norway and Iceland, primarily based villages within the east, middle, and west of Greenland. The Greenlandic society, as quickly as a part of the Kalmar Union in the 14th century along Iceland, Sweden, and Finland, later confronted seize with the useful resource of both the Norwegian Empire and the Danish.

The improvement of North Greenlandic paralleled that of Icelandic and Faroese but diverged from the Scandinavian languages spoken at the European continent. The colony have turn out to be an increasing number of isolated from the rest of the Nordic worldwide. Despite their linguistic uniqueness, the Greenlandic settlers faced disturbing conditions as environmental situations shifted, and Greenland have end up reduce off from the traditional agricultural practices of the Nordic location.

The Norse exploration did no longer end with Greenland; in 1080, Erik the Red expanded their horizons through the use of attaining the North American continent. While it stays manageable that the Norse explored regions farther south, definitive proof is however to be exposed. The Vikings' affect and gain extended beyond the recognized territories in their time.

In the overdue 14th and early 15th centuries, a dramatic drop in international temperatures supplied disturbing situations for the Greenlandic settlements. Villages confronted dwindling grain yields, prompting a shift within the route of dependence on fishing and whale looking. The harsh situations brought about hunger and freezing deaths maximum of the settlers, and in a few villages, the aged had been sacrificed during winters to maintain restrained meals resources.

Greenland discovered itself remoted from other Norse settlements because of freezing weather that rendered tour no longer possible. Despite the demanding conditions and closing dying of the Norse settlements, they made contact with the Inuit individuals who had displaced the Dorset peoples on the island.

The Slave Trade in Viking History

In the annals of Viking history, past the stories of bloodthirsty piracy, lies a lesser-diagnosed however massive aspect — that of slave trading. This narrative sheds moderate at the cruel practices of the Vikings in obtaining and buying and selling slaves, revealing a darker facet of their maritime exploits.

Viking Economy and Demand for Slaves

Contrary to famous mythology, change held a critical feature inside the Viking economy, as highlighted by means of way of way of medieval Arabic writers. The Vikings, lacking cultivated fields, sought slaves as rate from Eastern Slavic cities in Russia and Finnish agricultural villages. Simultaneously, they enslaved the local populations of invaded territories in France, Britain, and Ireland, weaving a complex internet of exploitation.

The Slavic people faced large enslavement, leaving an prolonged-lasting effect contemplated inside the English language, wherein the term "slave" originates from "Slavic." The Vikings orchestrated a scientific trade of slaves, transporting them to rich cities inside the Islamic worldwide, notably Baghdad, and using deceptive routes over Russian rivers.

Cruel Realities

Despite contemporaries noting mainly awesome treatment of slaves by using Vikings, it have become a practical rather than altruistic approach. Slaves, both male and woman, have been anticipated to engage in sexual circle of relatives contributors with their Viking masters. The seemingly humane remedy served the motive of retaining the slaves' physical situation and appearance, ensuring maximum rate while supplied for silver.

Widespread Slave Trade

The Viking involvement within the slave exchange have turn out to be no longer isolated; it spanned a broader European context. The Venetians, specifically, excelled inside the realm of slave trading, highlighting the pervasive nature of this exercise for the duration of medieval Europe.

Exploring Vinland

While the Viking Age bore witness to plunder and slaughter, it moreover marked an generation of discovery and boom.

Newfoundland, referred to as Vinland in Viking sagas, witnessed Viking agreement. Although brief-lived, the undertaking into Vinland opened the door to a speculative question: What if the Vikings had decided on to remain in North America? Considering the possibility of a parallel universe wherein the failed colony of Newfoundland thrived just like Iceland, the hypothetical state of affairs unfolds, tough historical trajectories and inviting contemplation at the destiny of Viking exploration in the New World.

In exploring the capability survival and colonization of Newfoundland via manner of Vikings, severa important elements emerge, contributing to the final dying of this Norse undertaking.

Encounters with Indigenous People

The preliminary task arose within the encounters the various Vikings and the indigenous humans, known as "Scraeling" with the aid of the usage of the use of the Norse. The strained courting added approximately violence, with indigenous human beings killed within the first stumble upon. The battle set the tone for an uneasy coexistence, diminishing the prospects of peaceful interplay the various Vikings and the close by population.

A huge obstacle to the sustained Viking presence in Newfoundland emerge as the populace dynamics. The Norse, outnumbered by means of way of countless others, faced the stark fact that large-scale settlement in Canada became now not possibly. The confined population in Scandinavia itself posed a capture 22 scenario to the envisioning of a thriving Viking colony in North America.

The 0.33 impediment lay within the technological barriers and navigational worrying situations faced with the useful resource of the Vikings. While their strengths lay in coastal waters, the danger of common tours to the New World, with its expansive seas, posed issues. The Vikings' navigational prowess did not usually growth seamlessly to broader maritime endeavors.

Contrary to visions of an possibility information wherein Vikings and community populations coexist harmoniously, ancient evidence indicates a specific narrative. The Vikings showed little interest in integrating with the indigenous people, and their restrained numbers hindered the formation of a sustainable society. The slow erosion of Scandinavian lifestyle in the colony foreshadowed its inevitable decline.

Considering the colonization and survival of Newfoundland as a theoretical achievement, the established order of a everlasting Scandinavian presence in Canada would hinge on the dissemination of this fulfillment. The hypothetical state of affairs envisions facts spreading, attracting more Vikings emigrate to North America.

The Decline and Fall of the Viking

Moving beyond the Newfoundland narrative, the decline of the Viking Empire within the eleventh century spread out amidst various factors. A super improvement have grow to be the developing political interest in Scandinavia, laying the inspiration for the current Scandinavian international locations.

The Vikings' structured splendor system, fostering opportunities for raiding, regularly shifted in the route of democratic rule. The emphasis on shared control—"we're all leaders proper proper here"—ultimately gave manner to a migration of the rich elite to better stages of presidency. This shift led to more centralized control and the convergence of the previous Viking homelands with the wider European political panorama.

In a first-rate transformation, the Norse people underwent cultural adjustments in the course of a period marked through the conversion to Christianity and a slowing pace of Viking expeditions.

Christianity acquired ground in Viking-occupied lands, with missionary Leif Erikson gambling a crucial feature inside the conversion machine. The as quickly as steadfast opposition to Christianity weakened, critical to the tremendous adoption of the ultra-modern faith at some point of Scandinavian nations.

While the Vikings had previously seized notable expanses of the northwestern global, their expeditions steadily slowed. Following their expulsion from North America inside the one year a thousand, the Vikings avoided sending settlers to what they perceived as a foreign places and strange region.

Greenland, too, confronted an inevitable disintegrate. Isolated from the relaxation of Europe for hundreds of years, the Greenland colony succumbed to excessive weather conditions. The dispersion of Greenland's Norse populace have become an unusual phenomenon, brought about by way of a couple of factors because the colonies had been abandoned via the fifteenth century.

The nature of Europe have become present manner tremendous adjustments, making it an increasing number of hard for the Vikings to launch a achievement expeditions. Countries like England and France set up eternal, professional armies, fortifying their willing cities in response to Viking incursions. This shift inside the European political and military panorama in addition contributed to the decline of Viking have an impact on.

The Viking Age approached its end with the sick-fated attempt of Earl Totsig Godwinson to rule Northumbria. Facing a rebellion and next exile from England, he sought alliance with Norway's King Herald Hardrada, fundamental to a statement of struggle in opposition to England's King Henry II in 1066. The sports that unfolded marked the very last financial ruin in the Viking technology.

As the Vikings misplaced territory and underwent mass conversions to Christianity, their religious and cultural practices began to wane. The decline of Viking civilization modified into hastened with the resource of the usage of the growing have an impact on of Christianity, which supplanted pagan traditions across Europe. This technique, but, spread out step by step, taking about centuries for Christianity to emerge as the dominant religion in Scandinavia after the defeat of the Vikings.

After the Viking Age, historians penned famous Norse sagas, chronicling the humans and occasions that original Viking civilization. The reliability of extraordinary stories stays dubious, as bills have been often stimulated with the useful resource of Christian biases and views of these whose lands have been raided by way of using the Vikings.

The records of the Vikings is each unusual and enigmatic, with remarkable a restricted amount of verifiable records preserved from their amazing civilization. Despite the uncertainties, the Norse legacy has left an indelible mark on Western way of life, with Thursday nonetheless referred to as Thor's Day. Although the Viking Age has ended, the reminiscence of those feared and savage warriors persists in historic narratives and cultural affects.

Chapter 13: The Viking Encounter With Christianity

In the sector of religious transformation, the Vikings, now not like Charlemagne's compelled conversions, often embraced Christianity without resorting to the sword. During the early Viking Age, the shift in the direction of Christianity in Viking corporations has come to be inspired with the aid of manner of monetary troubles.

Merchants, keen to everyday rich change with Christian opposite numbers, determined that adherence to the Christian faith facilitated monetary dealings. It wasn't uncommon for a Viking provider company to seamlessly transition among the symbols of Thor's hammer and the Christian flow into, training every faiths without formal baptism.

Initially proof towards the new religion, the Norse Vikings clung to their pagan gods, content material with their historical beliefs. From the 700s to the 800s, Christian clergymen and clergymen launched into missionary journeys to Viking territories, laying the seeds of spiritual trade. However, the conversion of the Vikings spread out step by step over centuries. Even as Viking kings declared their kingdoms Christian, many Danes and Swedes persisted in pagan rituals. It modified into not till the near of the Viking Age that almost all of Vikings embraced Christianity, gift way baptism and Christian burials.

Christianization Across Viking Territories

Denmark's Christianization received momentum with the conversion of King Harald Bluetooth in 965. Despite an in advance baptism of Viking monarch Harald Klak in 826, large Christianization took time. Harald Bluetooth's assertion at the Jelling Stone proclaiming the conversion of all Danes did no longer proper now alter the spiritual landscape. Construction of Denmark's first stone church in Ribe started out around 1110, symbolizing the gradual transition to Christianity. By 1134, even as the church emerge as finished, the bulk of Danes had embraced the Christian faith.

In Norway, Olaf Tryggvason played a pivotal function in bringing Christianity to the main side. His splendid riot in competition to the pagan king Hakkon Jarl in 995 marked a turning detail. While earlier rulers had embraced Christianity, Olaf resorted to coercion to position into effect conversion, dismantling pagan shrines and the usage of force towards Vikings immune to the new religion. Norway, beneath such immoderate measures, underwent a forced Christianization, and Olaf's efforts are credited with the Christianization of Iceland and specific Western Islands.

The eleventh century witnessed the reputation quo of Episcopal sees in Sweden, signaling the graduation of Christianity's expansion inside the route of the late Viking Age. Sweden's conversion end up marked with the beneficial resource of warfare and brutality, coexisting with pagan traditions for a time. Many Swedish Vikings favored a gradual shift to Christianity on the equal time as preserving elements in their antique religion. By the 12th century, however, the bulk of Swedes had embraced Christianity, finishing the Christianization of Viking territories.

Viking Society

Within the confines of a predominantly male society, Viking women wielded a big diploma of have an impact on. While guys engaged in sports sports which include raiding, fishing, exploring, or change, Viking girls now not only controlled traditional obligations however also took on roles deemed specific to men. The society fantastically valued girls, and assaulting them became socially stigmatized.

The each day lives of Viking girls revolved spherical multifaceted responsibilities. Apart from project family chores like cooking, cleaning, and infant-rearing, they had been tasked with gardening, keeping food for wintry climate, and crafting clothing for the own family. The difficult work-in depth technique of spinning, carding, weaving, slicing, and stitching must soak up to 35 hours to provide enough yarn for a unmarried day's weaving.

Marriage in Viking society have become a huge event usually arranged thru the mother and father of the engaged couple. It have come to be not in reality a union of individuals but a settlement among households. The groom's own family paid a bride rate throughout betrothal, even as the bride's family provided a dowry inside the route of the bridal ceremony. Marriage held monetary implications for every devices of dad and mom, adding a layer of complexity past the couple's happiness.

Unlike modern education, Viking kids did not attend formal institutions. Instead, know-how became exceeded down interior households. Sons positioned from their fathers and uncles, inheriting talents related to their change, at the same time as daughters had been taught domestic responsibilities thru their mothers and aunts. By the a long term of 12 to 15, every boys and women received the maturity and capabilities crucial to govern circle of relatives and farm obligations.

Though adhering to large social norms, Viking girls exhibited exceptions, specifically in some unspecified time in the destiny of exploration and agreement. Women accompanied guys on journeys to new lands, together with Iceland, Greenland, and Vinland. In instances of emigration to Britain, Ireland, and France, however, men commonly engaged in raids and commerce, on the same time as women remained at domestic coping with familial domains.

In assessment to medieval Europe, Viking ladies loved greater autonomy. They possessed felony avenues to dissolve marriages, acquire land, and set up agencies. Some girls accrued wealth as landowners, and archaeological reveals, together with scales in tombs, recommend their involvement in exchange. While maximum girls operated inside the familial realm, some ventured beyond, participating in various factors of Viking society.

Merchant Ventures of the Vikings

In the expansive Viking Age beginning within the 790s, the Vikings launched into trips now not totally for plunder however to set up and find out new alternate routes. Seeking strong property of profits, many Vikings sought or initiated change routes to places like Newfoundland inside the west and Constantinople inside the east, navigating the Volga River and its tributaries. Emigration styles numerous, with Swedish person person men predominantly settling in Russia, even as Norwegians and Danes decided houses inside the British Isles and France.

During the ones voyages, Vikings engaged in bartering for necessities, shopping for and promoting northern products which incorporates fur, amber, iron, and walrus tusks. Slave change also became a commodity of their commercial employer sports sports. The Vikings' ventures extended to the New World and Eastern territories, showcasing their prowess no longer simply in raids however moreover in setting up tricky alternate networks.

Along the coastlines of Europe, the Vikings had been no longer completely raiders but moreover ambitious investors and settlers. For three centuries, church homes prayed to be spared the "wrath of the Norsemen," who engaged in every commercial transactions and army raiding.

Unprotected church buildings and monasteries confronted their attacks, while properly-defended settlements became worthwhile trading places. Early within the Viking Age, barter emerge as the usual exchange technique, but as time improved, Viking investors amassed exchange silver and Arabic cash to facilitate their purchases.

Dublin, Ireland, and York, England, emerged as permanent Viking settlements and pivotal buying and selling facilities. These hubs no longer simplest attracted distant places exchange however moreover housed Viking artisans who crafted an array of products, which incorporates combs from bone and antler, leather-based-primarily based gadgets, rings, textiles, guns, and armor. The Viking presence in those regions precipitated a fusion of cultures, putting in an enduring settlement.

Throughout the Viking Age, Norsemen installed settlements alongside Europe's coastlines. They invaded Normandy in France, colonized southern Italy, and claimed Atlantic islands which encompass Orkney, Shetland, the Hebrides, Scilly, and the Isle of Man. These Viking settlers intermingled with nearby populations, contributing to the arrival of eternal agencies in the place.

Eastern Trade

While Vikings traditionally traded inside the Baltic Sea vicinity, the 8th century saw an growth into Russia to discover worthwhile shopping for and promoting routes. Predominantly Swedes, with a few Danes and Norwegians, Vikings navigated rivers just like the Dnieper and Volga to advantage the Black Sea and Caspian Sea, respectively. Establishing towns and shopping for and selling posts, which includes Novgorod and Kiev, Vikings engaged in alternate with the Volga Bulgars, later called the Rus. Slavery done a large feature in Viking exchange, with slaves acquired from raids and wars locating markets in Constantinople and Baghdad.

Chapter 14: Games And Entertainment

Amidst their campaigns for conquest and looking for and selling endeavors, the Vikings decided solace in a plethora of games and amusements, showcasing a colorful trouble of their lifestyle. Grave items and sagas unveil a spectrum of sports activities enjoyed via way of the usage of Vikings at some stage in feasts and gatherings, starting from board video games and cube video video games to playing and bodily sports sports activities.

Hnefatafl, a strategic board mission, received popularity for the duration of Greenland, Iceland, Scotland, Ireland, and Great Britain, originating from Scandinavia. Although specifics approximately the game's rules are scarce, it concerned game enthusiasts with choppy abilties, growing a fascinating dynamic. The monarch defended a fortress with a smaller army, aiming to trap the opponent inner. The Viking Age noticed the zenith of hnefatafl's popularity until the advent of chess inside the twelfth century introduced approximately its decline.

Indoor sports featured eating video video games, often regarding companies of ladies and men. After imbibing, contributors engaged in conceited statements, rhymes, and playful insults, tough the opposing enterprise to outdrink and outinsult them. Post-meal entertainment blanketed dice rolling, making a song, and storytelling, highlighting the Vikings' penchant for merriment.

Outdoor sports activities have been in addition famous, showcasing the bodily prowess of Viking warriors. Tournaments featured archery, wrestling, stone hurling, swordplay, and stallion fights, where horses engaged in combat. Sports like wrestling, toga-honk (a form of tug-of-struggle), sprinting, swimming, and a ball game with stick and ball furnished more avenues for pastime. However, the hard nature of Viking play often brought approximately accidents and even deaths, witnessed with the useful resource of spectators, together with girls.

Viking dad and mom crafted wood toys for their youngsters, who engaged in sports like playing with balls and adapting adult games to in shape their age. Miniature versions of swords, shields, and spears located in burials pondered the incorporation of play into the Viking toddler's world, contributing to the broader expertise of Viking life past warfare and raiding.

The Rich Artistic Legacy

The paintings of the Vikings stands as a testament to the tough material way of lifestyles of Northern Europeans. Vikings adorned now not handiest their weapons and jewellery however moreover runestones and supply's woodwork with complicated decorations. Embracing multilined, summary animal motifs, their art work featured snakes, horses, wolves, birds, and fantastical beasts.

Evolving through six awesome however interconnected modern moves, the geographic beginning of an object decided its decorative fashion. From seen expressions on runestones to complex deliver carvings, the Vikings left a protracted-lasting mark on the creative panorama, showcasing the severa sides in their innovative spirit.

Weapons and Armor

In the sector of Viking weaponry and armor, the first rate developments of the society need to be taken into consideration. Adult free grownup guys in Viking way of life, adhering to an honor-centric ethos, constantly saved a weapon indoors achieve, frequently suspending them near their drowsing quarters. Preparedness for warfare, whether or not or not in feuds or duels, have become ingrained inside the Viking manner of existence.

While severa fingers inclusive of swords, sax (brief swords), axes, spears, bows and arrows, shields, helmets, and chainmail had been available, the rate of iron, a valuable beneficial useful resource, stimulated their accessibility. Only the wealthiest Vikings may additionally need to govern to pay for an entire set of hands, with even the poorest making sure they possessed an awl, spear, and guard, frequently repurposing tools from their each day farm life.

A strict hierarchy dominated the possession of guns, with slaves, women, and children expressly prohibited from sporting fingers. Free girls and children once in a while owned knives for farm use, but weaponry remained forbidden for slaves.

The sword, a image of reputation and wealth, stood because the maximum highly-priced opportunity because of the sizable quantity of iron required for its production. Typically double-edged with a median duration of 35 inches, these prized swords had been often pattern-welded, developing a superb appearance. Vibrant names like Blood-hungry and Leg-biter brought individual to those weapons, slung over the shoulders and gripped geared up in the right palms.

Axes and spears located more commonplace utilization among Viking men. Battle axes, with numerous head sizes and office paintings, have been ambitious guns stated for their devastating impact. Elaborate carving adorned each axe and sword blades, with a few, similar to the 971 Mammen awl, even offering gold and silver inlay. Spears, probable the most drastically used weapon, served every thrusting and throwing features, boasting various head designs.

Every Viking man wielded a spherical guard, with the protecting armament at once related to his wealth. Wealthier humans may additionally furthermore private chainmail and a steel helmet, every products of complicated craftsmanship and useful resource funding. Helmets, together with iron bowls with nostril guards, aimed to defend the pinnacle, even as those without get admission to to chainmail relied on thick, padded leather-based clothes.

Viking shields, extending as plenty as at least one meter in width, had been crafted through the use of becoming a member of wood forums in the center, presenting a handhold. Some shields showcased difficult artwork depicting mythological scenes or complex designs. These defensive measures, blended with primary but robust weapons, fueled the Viking conquests throughout England, France, and Russia, solidifying their popularity as bold warriors cast thru labor and combat fury.

The Viking Legal System

In the era of the Vikings, in which rune writing and oral tradition prevailed, a purposeful crook device and management existed, even without written laws. In each Viking community, a assembly known as the Thing served as a legal assembly wherein all man or woman men participated in law introduction and dispute choice. Each network had its first-rate Thing, contributing to a various jail panorama.

The Thing aimed to codify Viking regulation and settle disputes, steering some distance from reliance on duels or blood feuds. These gatherings had been scheduled at unique durations, and a law speaker from every Thing might recite the regulation verbatim. While all unfastened adult person males had a voice, the regulation speaker and neighborhood chieftain held the very last say in disputes, regularly endorsed through prominent households inside the area.

www.ingramcontent.com/pod-product-compliance
Lightning Source LLC
Chambersburg PA
CBHW071445080526
44587CB00014B/1994